MW01581529

SHAKA ZULU

He Who United the Tribes
Biography for Kids 9-12
Children's Biography Books

BABY PROFESSOR
EDUCATION KIDS

Speedy Publishing LLC
40 E. Main St. #1156
Newark, DE 19711
www.speedypublishing.com
Copyright 2017

All Rights reserved. No part of this book may be reproduced or used in any way or form or by any means whether electronic or mechanical, this means that you cannot record or photocopy any material ideas or tips that are provided in this book

In this book, we're going to talk about the life of Shaka Zulu. So, let's get right to it!

WHO WAS SHAKA ZULU?

Shaka Zulu was the powerful king and military leader of the Zulus from 1816 to 1828. He is known for bringing the diverse Zulu tribes together into one unified kingdom. The Zulus are a large group of native people who live in Southern Africa and who speak the Bantu language.

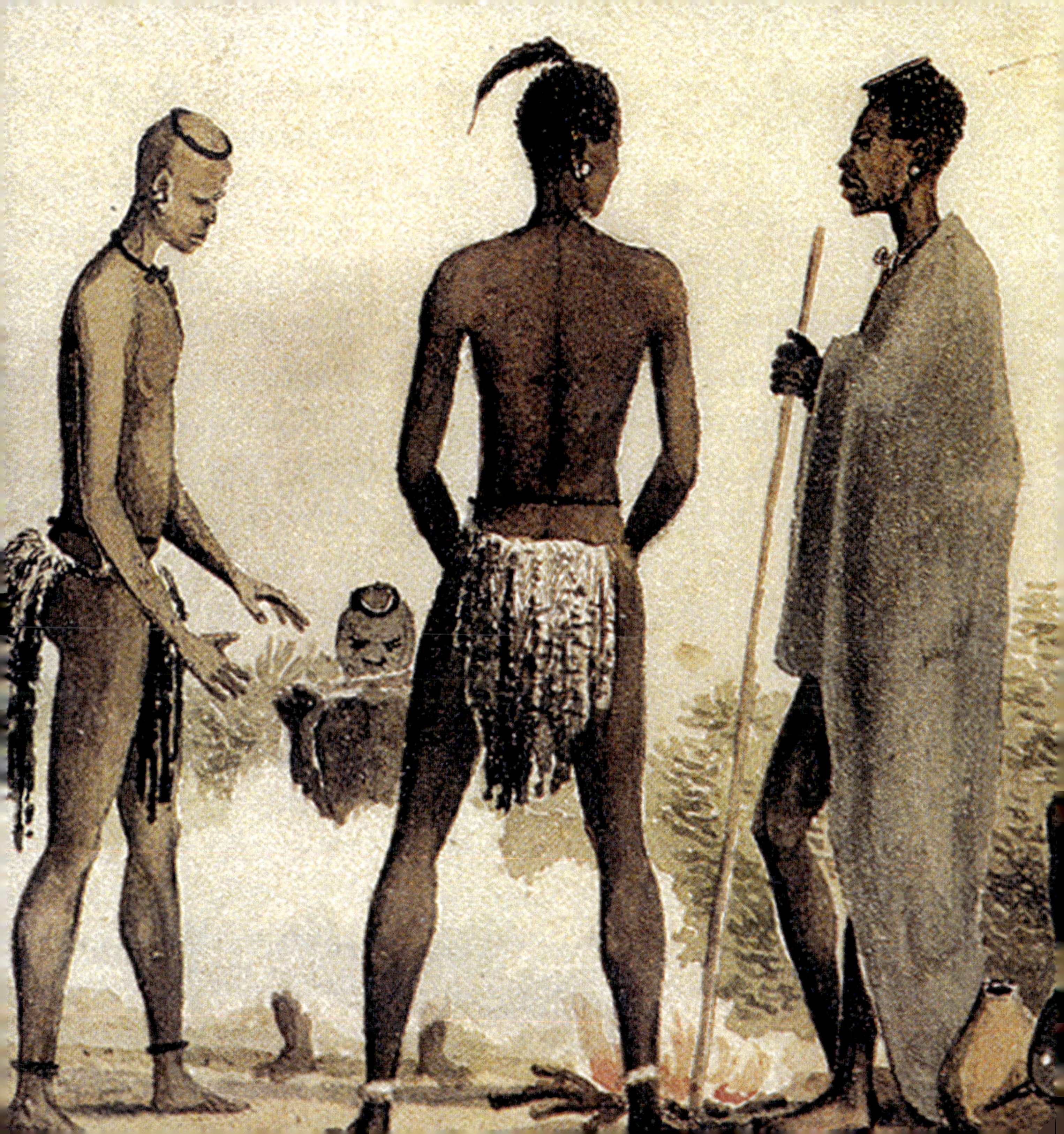

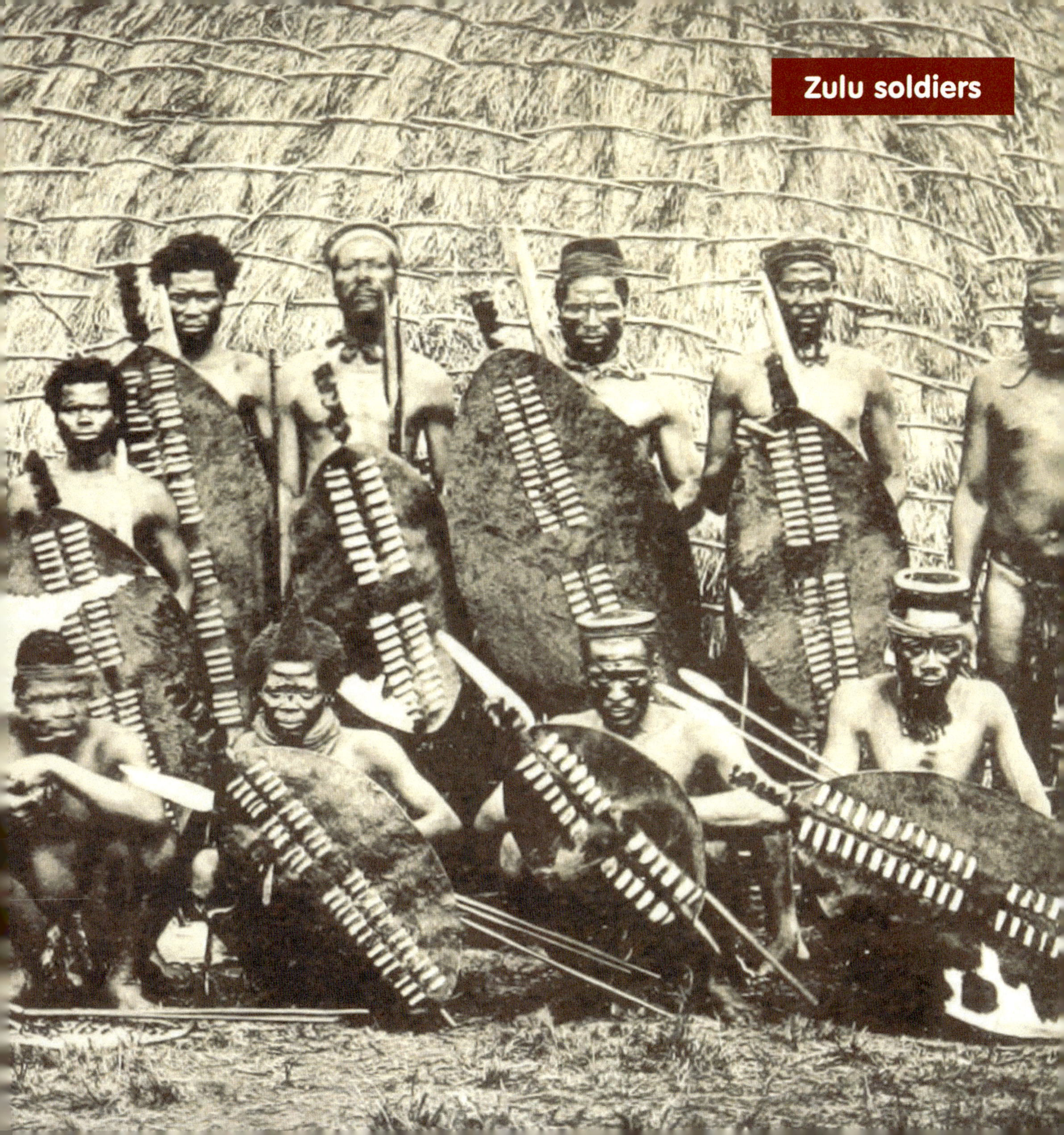
Zulu soldiers

EARLY LIFE

Shaka's father was a Zulu chief with the complicated name of Senzangakhona kaJama. He and Shaka's mother, named Nandi, weren't married when Nandi got pregnant. She was the daughter of a neighboring tribal chief.

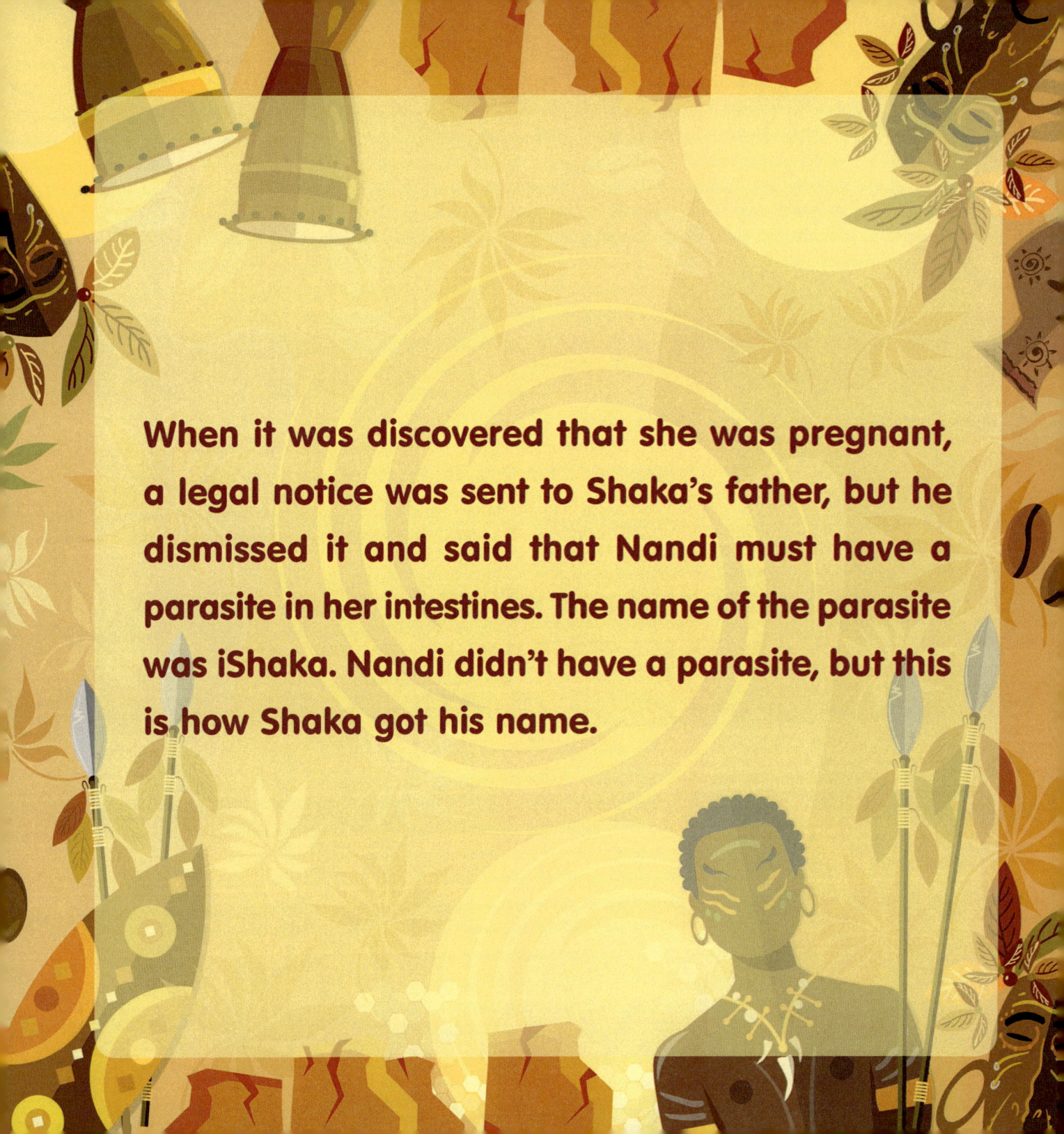

When it was discovered that she was pregnant, a legal notice was sent to Shaka's father, but he dismissed it and said that Nandi must have a parasite in her intestines. The name of the parasite was iShaka. Nandi didn't have a parasite, but this is how Shaka got his name.

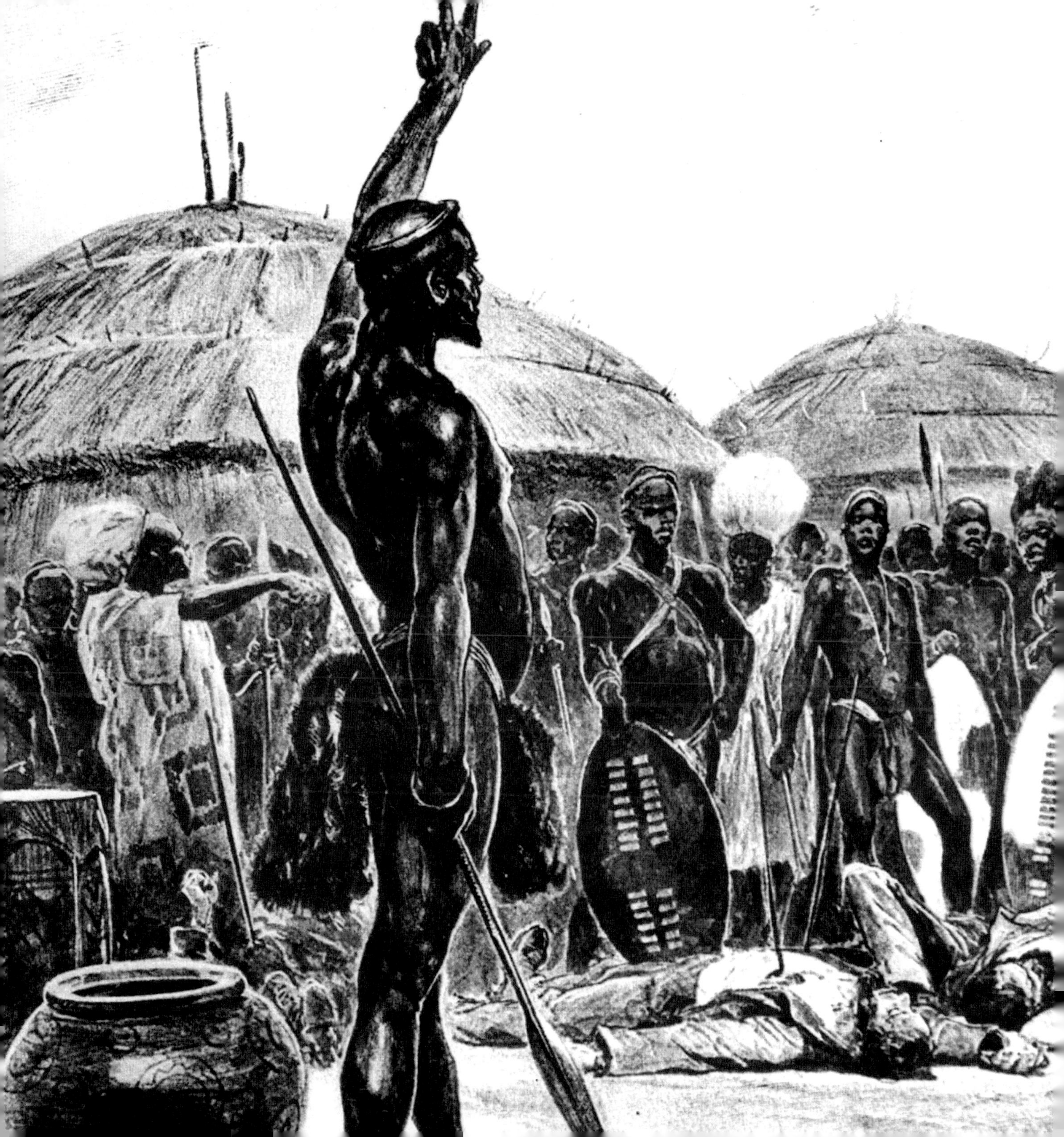

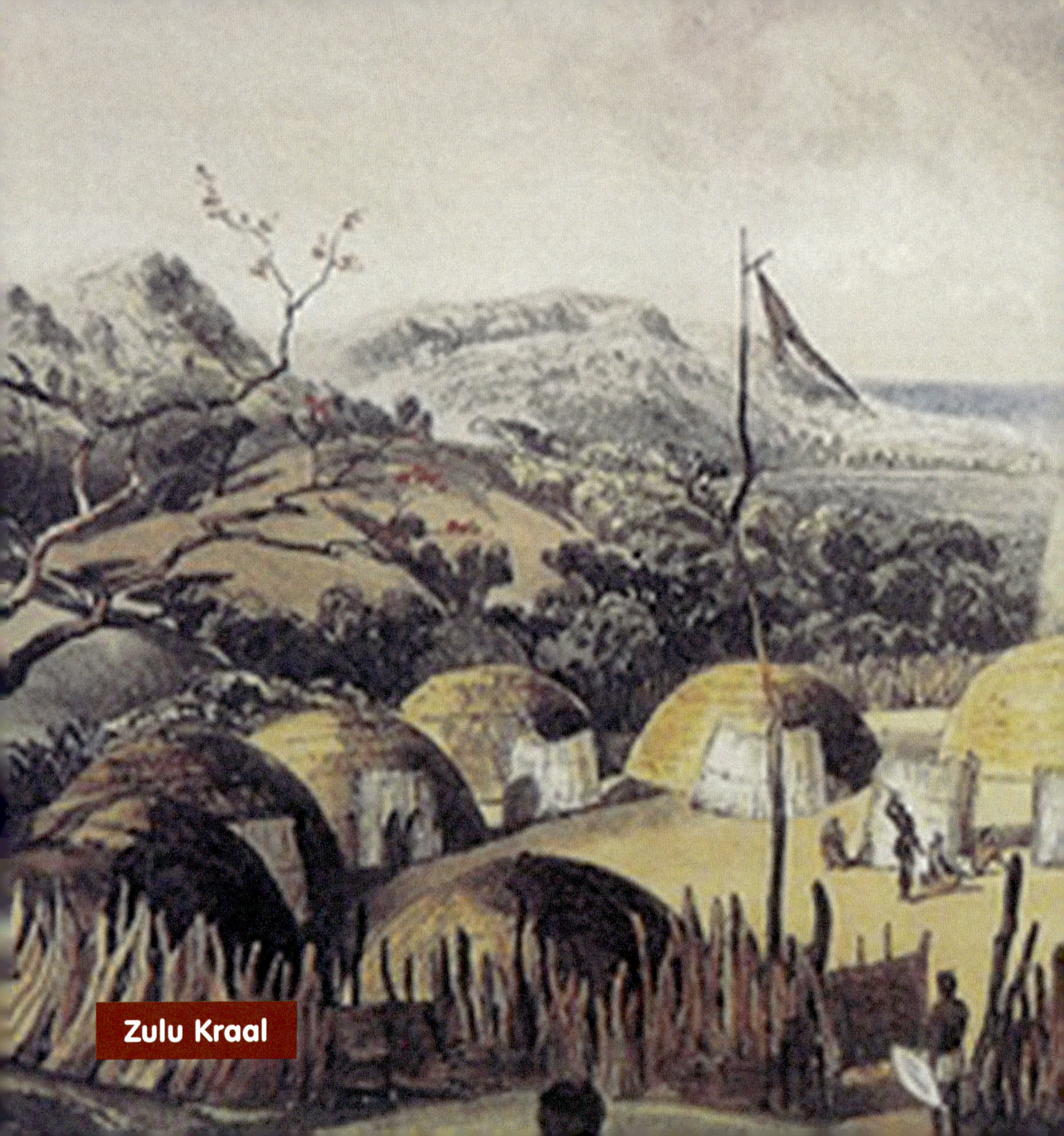

Zulu Kraal

As soon as Shaka was old enough, he was asked to shepherd his father's herd of sheep. When a wild dog attacked and killed one of the sheep, Shaka was blamed and his father banished him and his mother from their village, which was a town of huts called a kraal.

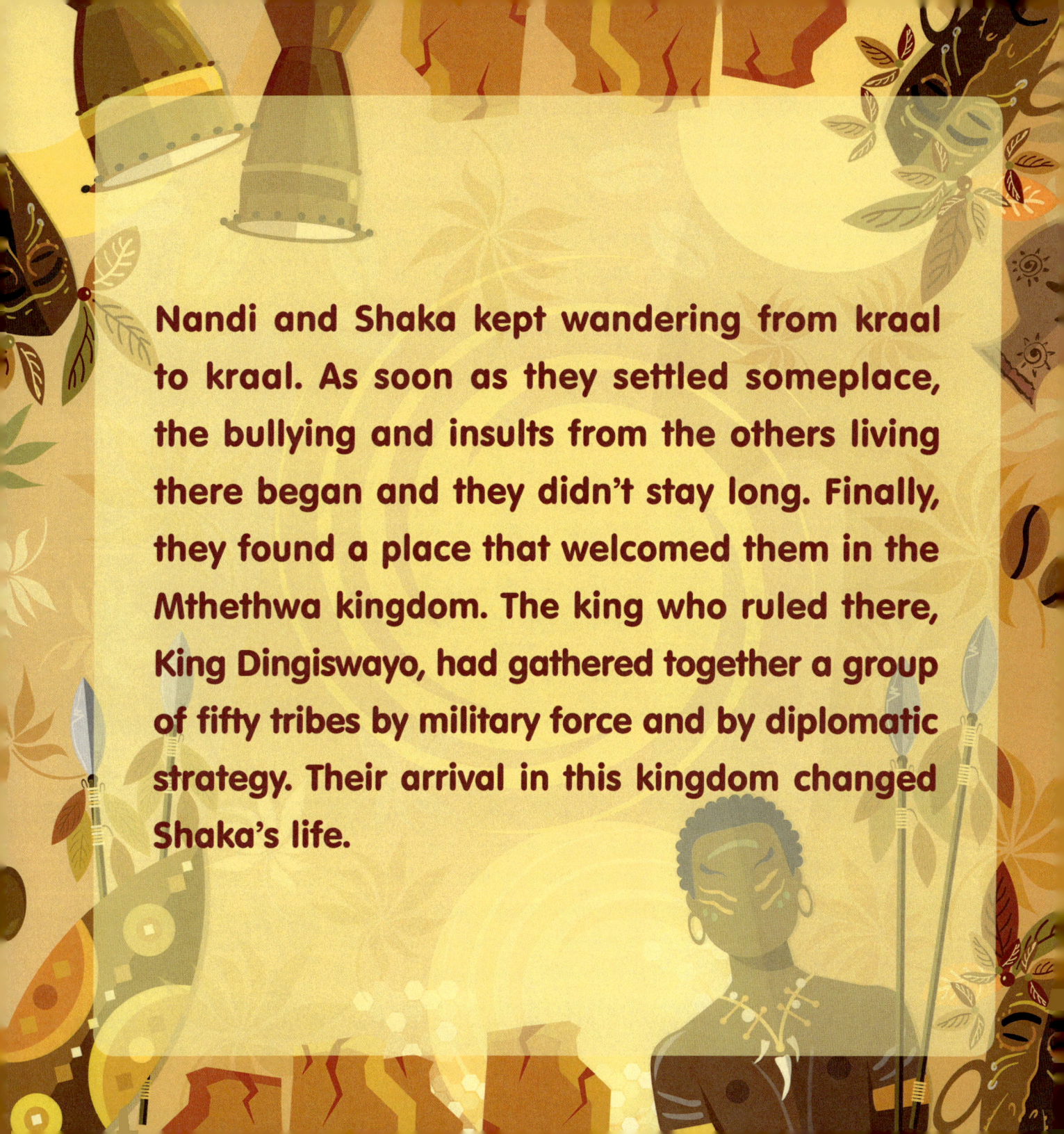

Nandi and Shaka kept wandering from kraal to kraal. As soon as they settled someplace, the bullying and insults from the others living there began and they didn't stay long. Finally, they found a place that welcomed them in the Mthethwa kingdom. The king who ruled there, King Dingiswayo, had gathered together a group of fifty tribes by military force and by diplomatic strategy. Their arrival in this kingdom changed Shaka's life.

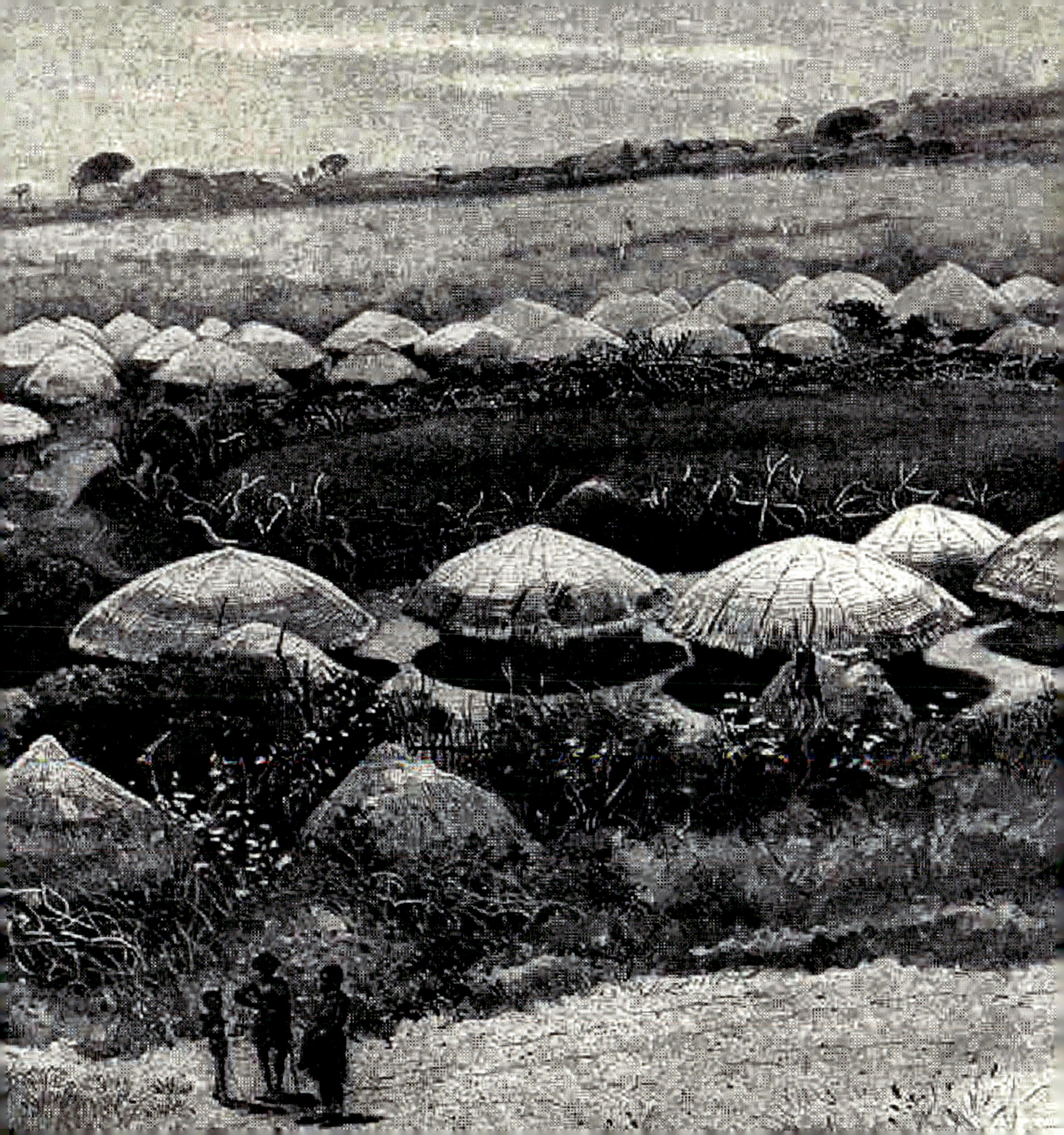

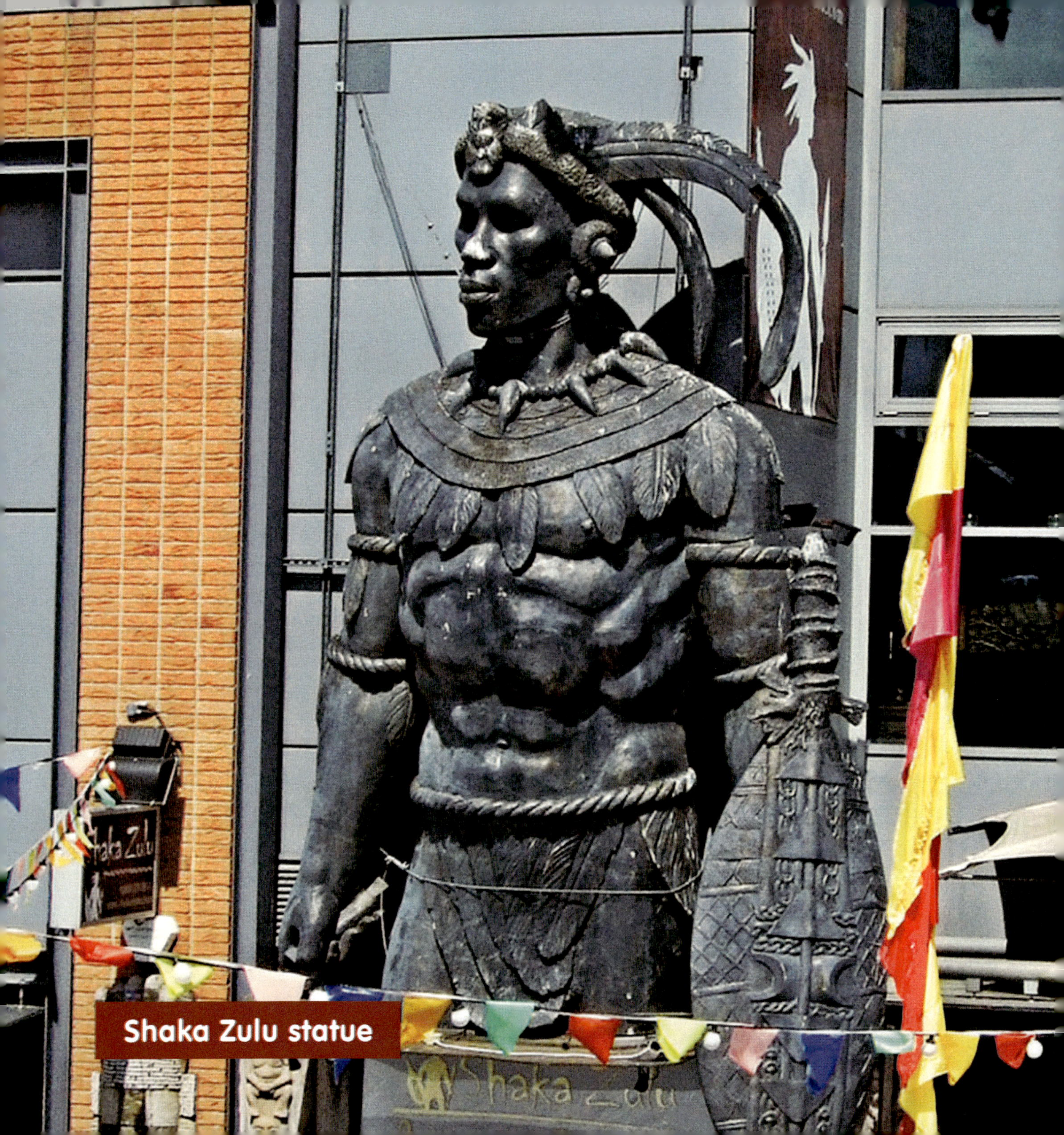
Shaka Zulu

Shaka Zulu statue

SHAKA THE WARRIOR

By the time he was a teenager, Shaka had become the king's major shepherd. He had learned his lesson from before and was not going to lose this opportunity. Once a leopard started to attack the flock and Shaka killed the beast by himself. The king rewarded him with words of praise and a highly valued cow.

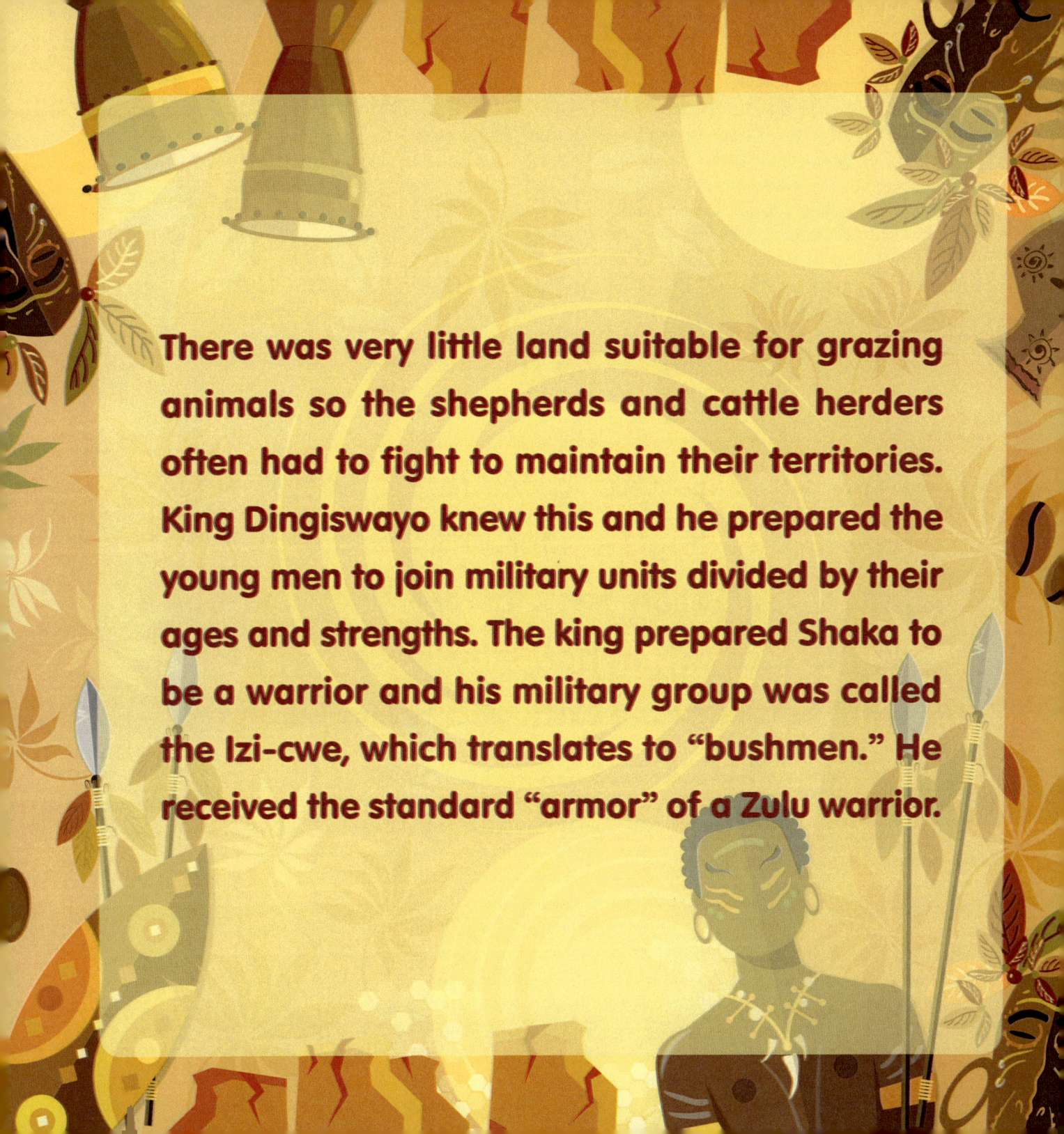

There was very little land suitable for grazing animals so the shepherds and cattle herders often had to fight to maintain their territories. King Dingiswayo knew this and he prepared the young men to join military units divided by their ages and strengths. The king prepared Shaka to be a warrior and his military group was called the Izi-cwe, which translates to "bushmen." He received the standard "armor" of a Zulu warrior.

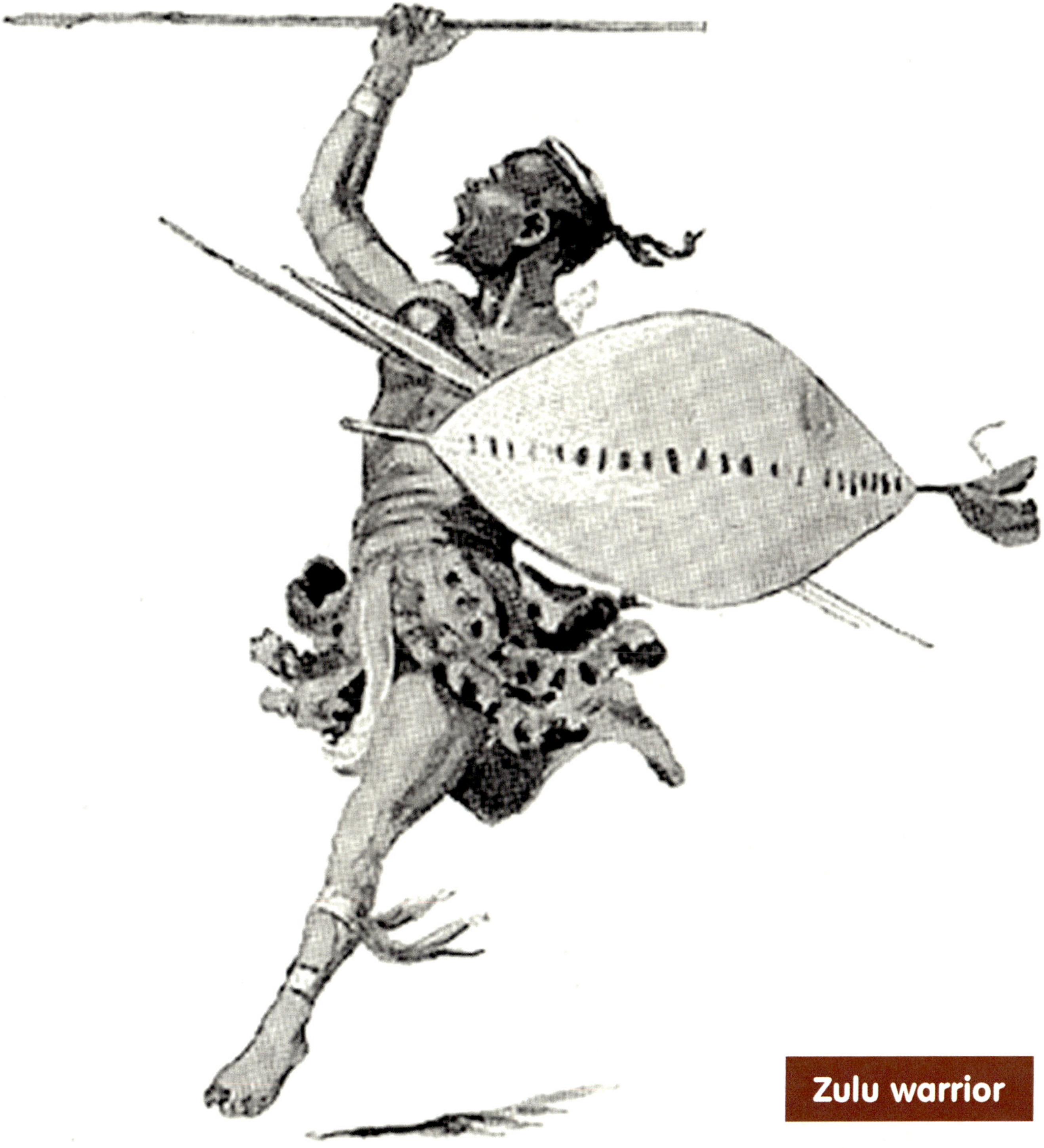

Zulu warrior

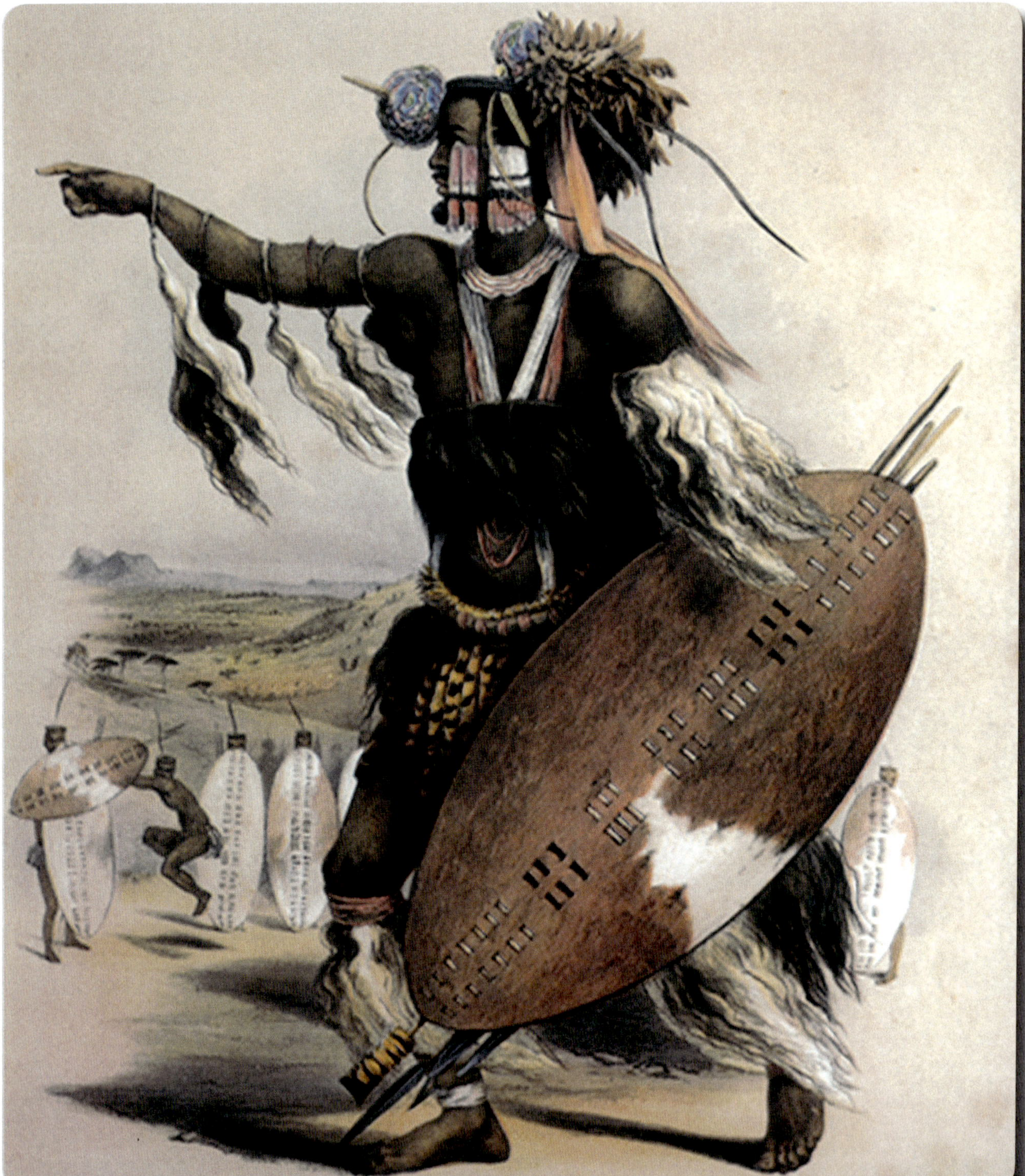

He had a shield that was oval in shape. He also had three spears for throwing. He wore a fur-striped kilt and a cape made of animal skin decorated with a bird's plumes. He was given sandals made from cowhide to wear and ceremonial oxtails to tie at his wrists and ankles. Armed with his weapons and military clothes and decorations, Shaka was ready for battle.

A NEW WAY TO FIGHT

At that time, the Zulus had a stylized way of fighting. The enemy groups of warriors would face off about 130 feet apart. Then they would throw their spears toward the enemy group.

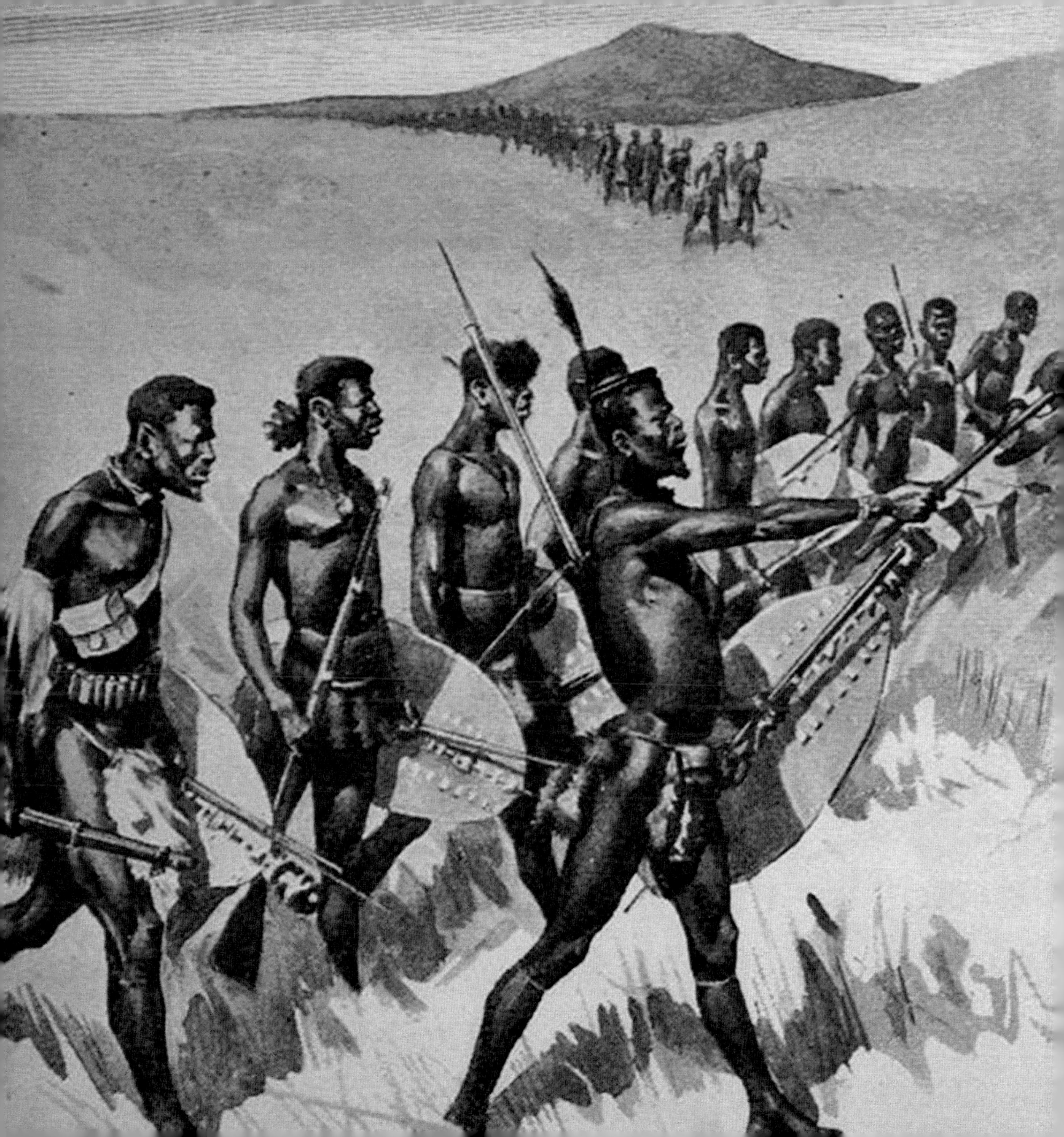

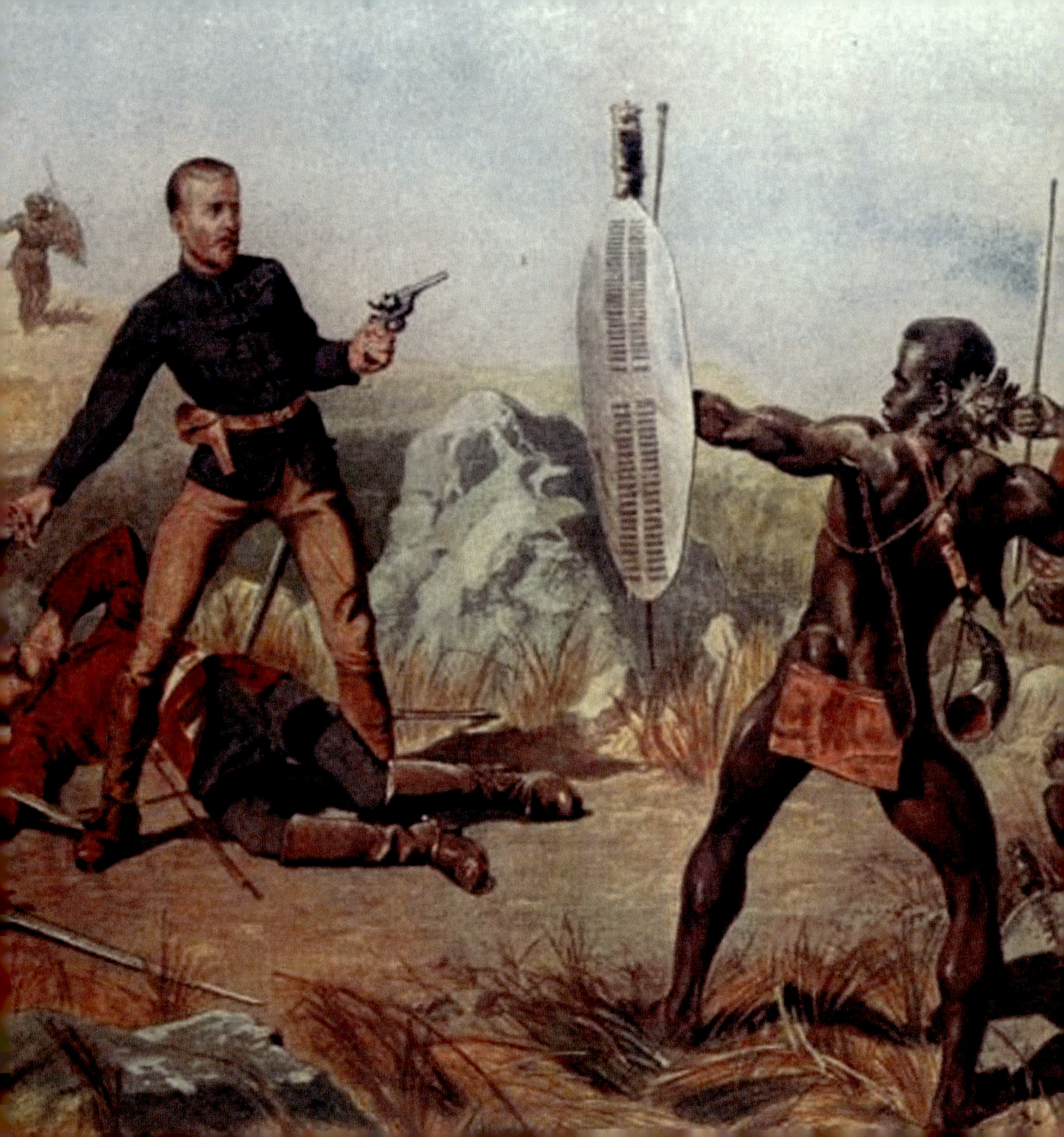

As a spear was thrown, another spear was thrown back in defense. When one side had had enough, they abandoned their weapons and fled. Shaka thought this way of fighting was totally pointless. Most of the time, the enemy wasn't hurt and lived to fight again.

Shaka started to change the way he was fighting. Instead of hurling spears at a distance, he engaged his enemy in hand-to-hand combat. When his enemy threw his spears, he would defend himself using his shield. Next, he charged forward hooking the shield of the enemy to his own. He then stabbed his opponent to death with a new type of short-handled spear he had invented and designed called an iklwa.

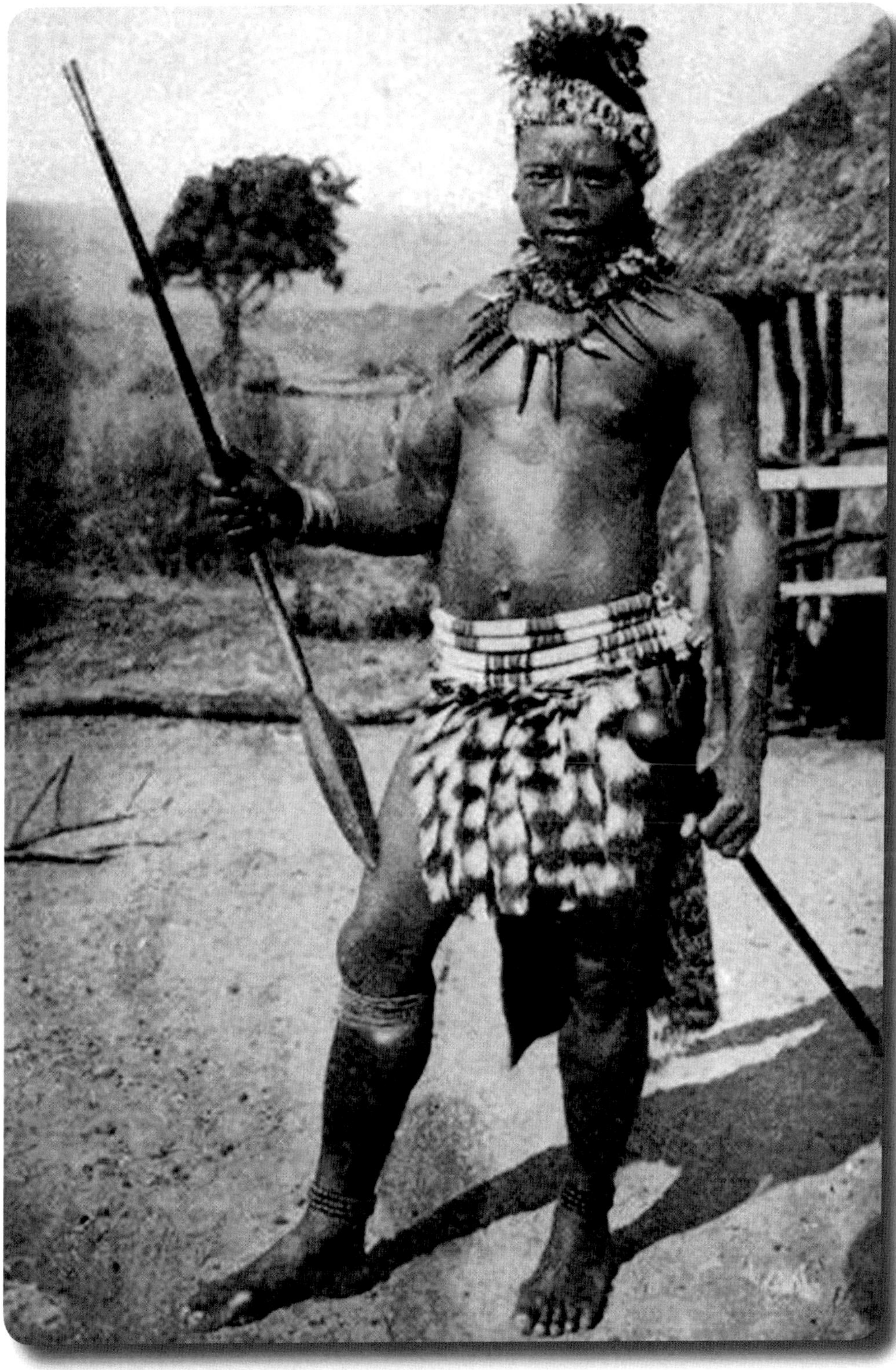

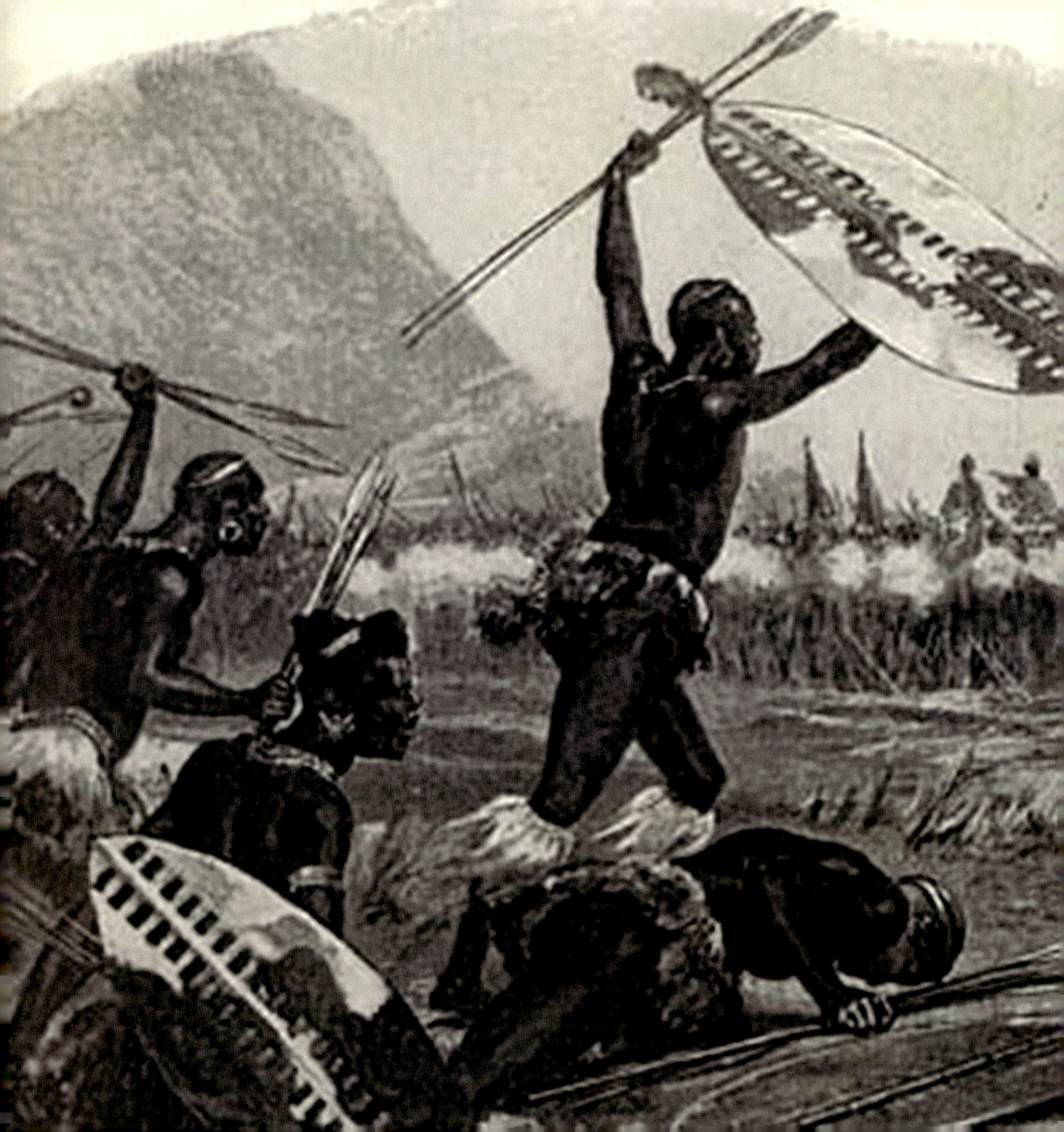

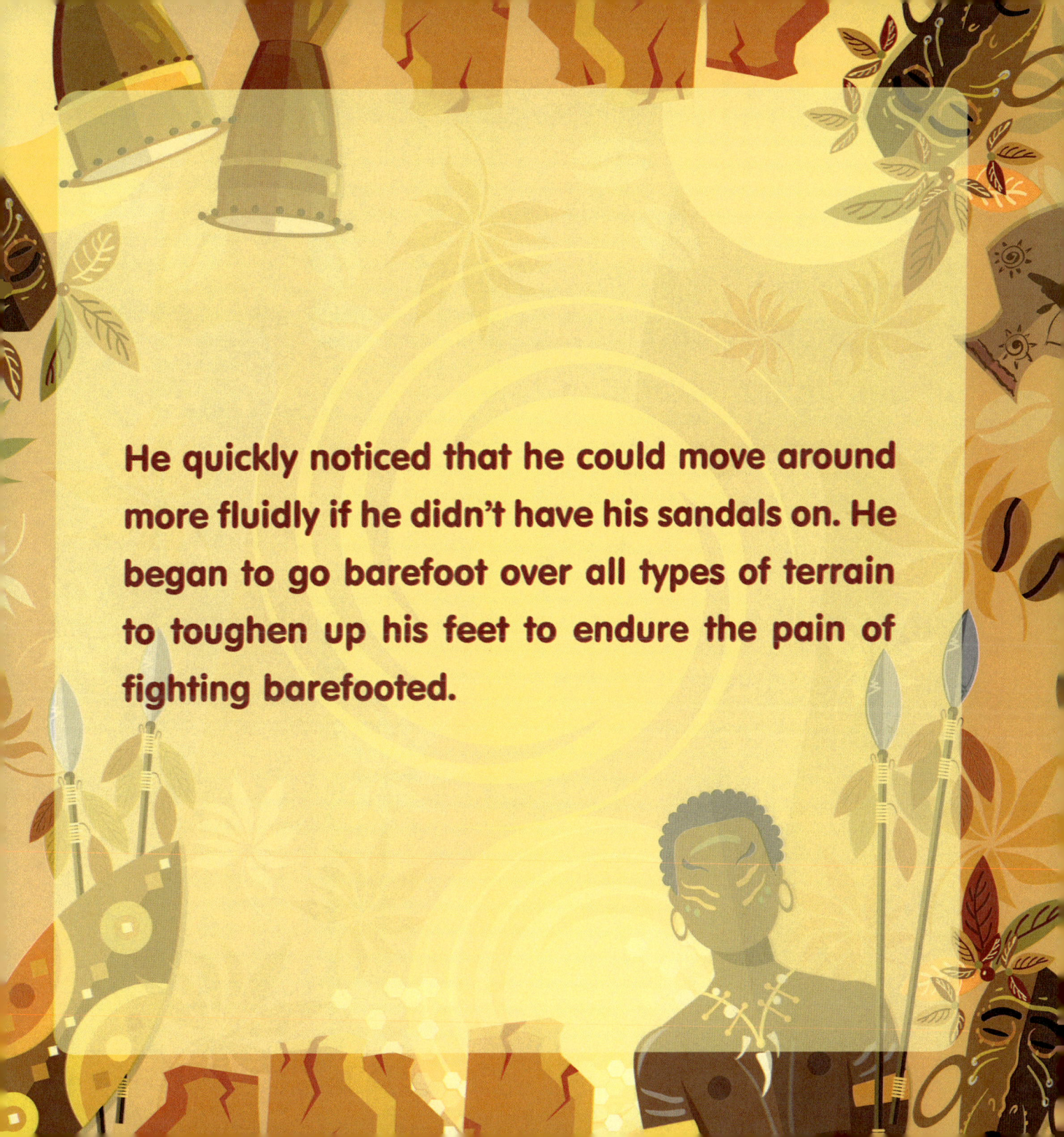

He quickly noticed that he could move around more fluidly if he didn't have his sandals on. He began to go barefoot over all types of terrain to toughen up his feet to endure the pain of fighting barefooted.

Shaka also organized his group of warriors into a different type of formation called "horns of the buffalo." In this formation, there was a main body of warriors for the buffalo's head. There were also two side-flanking forces that were like a buffalo's horns and the reserves that were like the animal's loins.

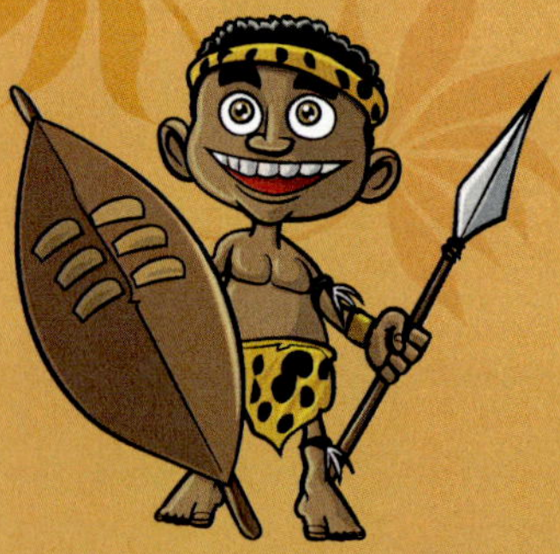

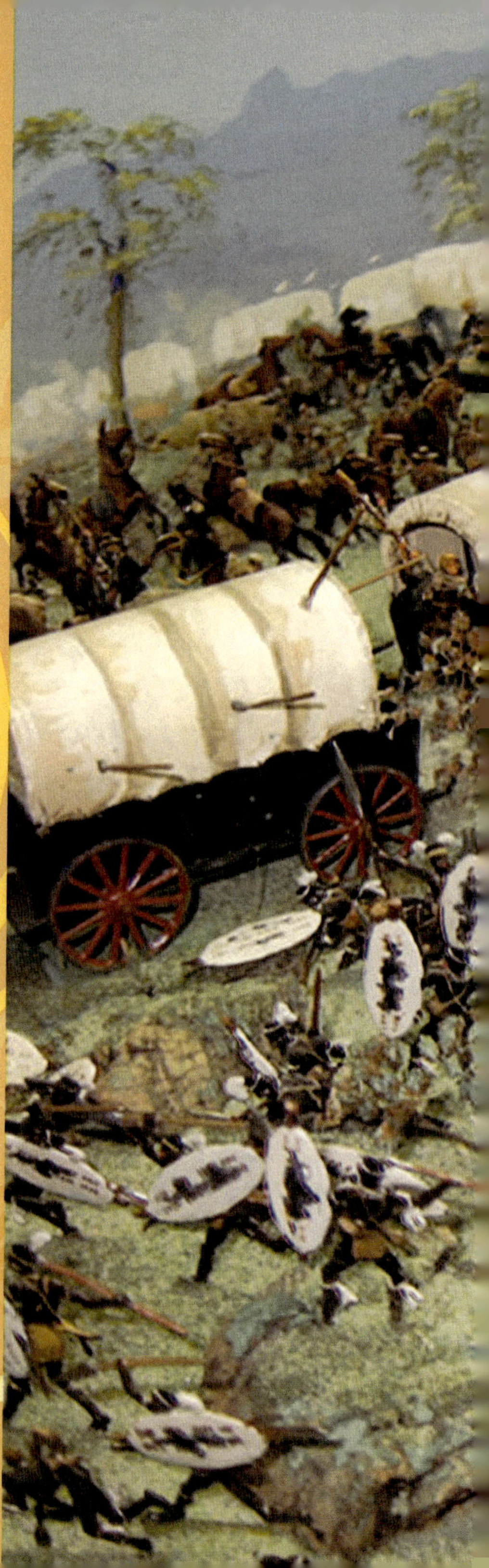

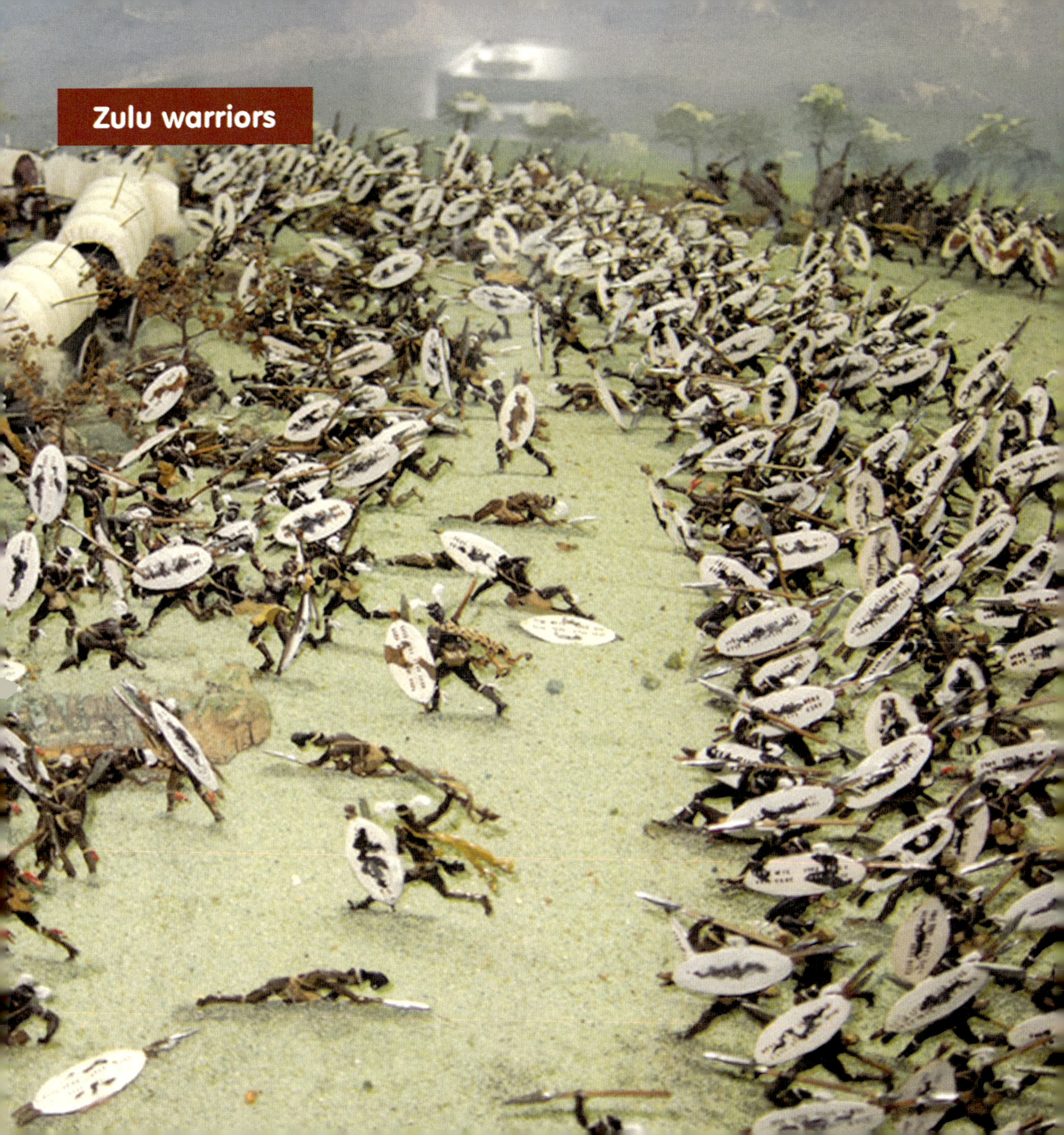
Zulu warriors

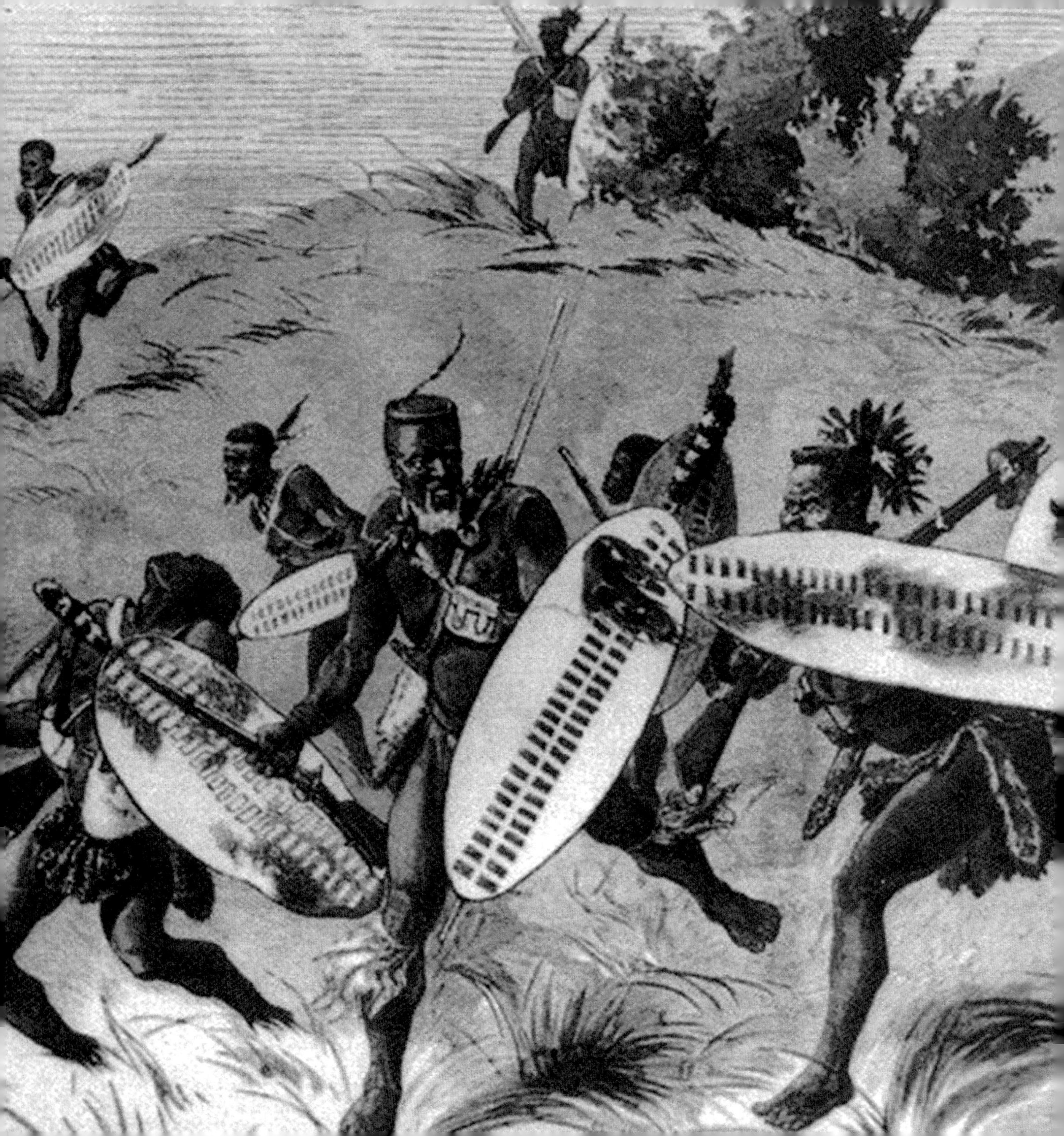

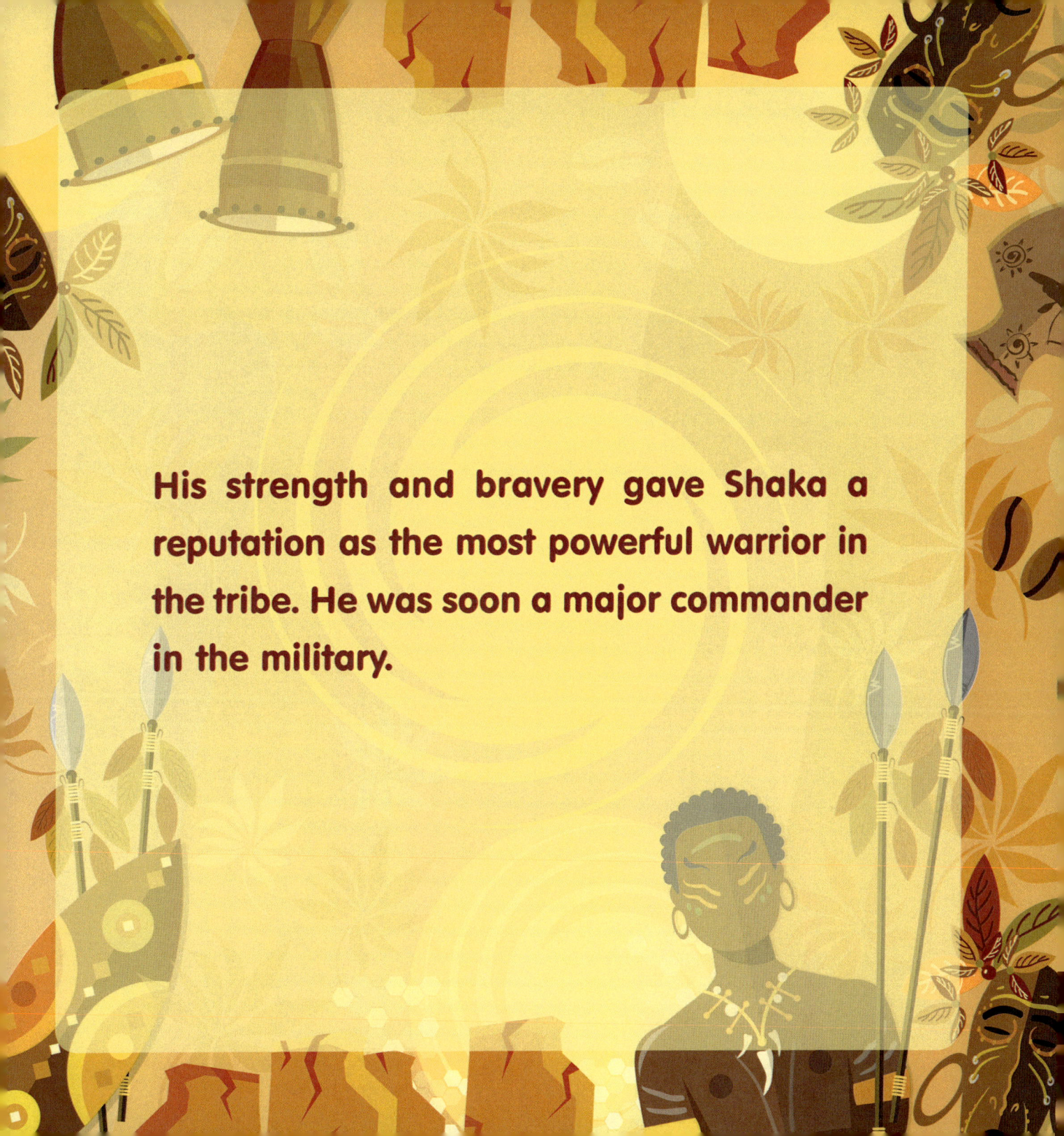

His strength and bravery gave Shaka a reputation as the most powerful warrior in the tribe. He was soon a major commander in the military.

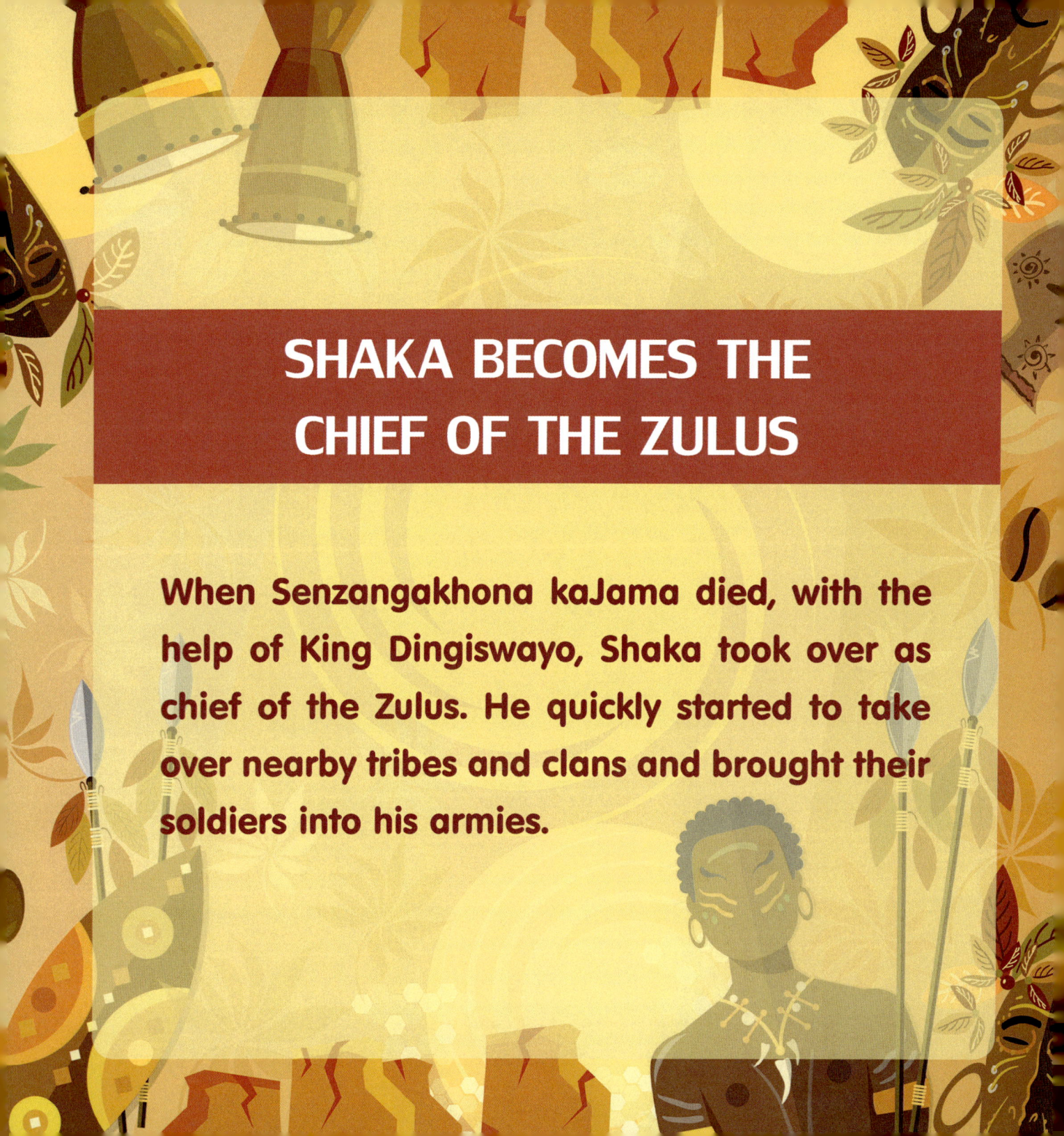

SHAKA BECOMES THE CHIEF OF THE ZULUS

When Senzangakhona kaJama died, with the help of King Dingiswayo, Shaka took over as chief of the Zulus. He quickly started to take over nearby tribes and clans and brought their soldiers into his armies.

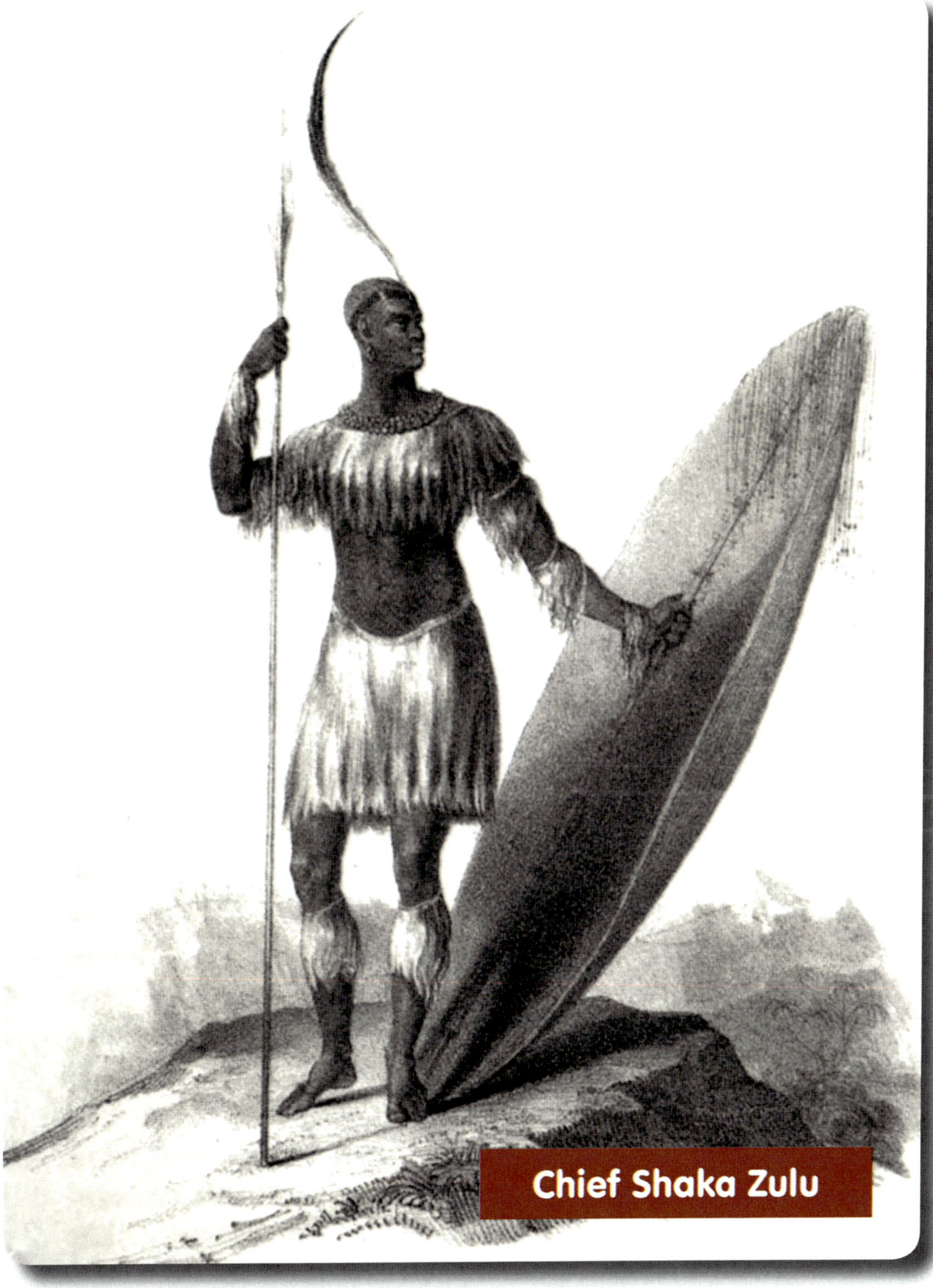

Chief Shaka Zulu

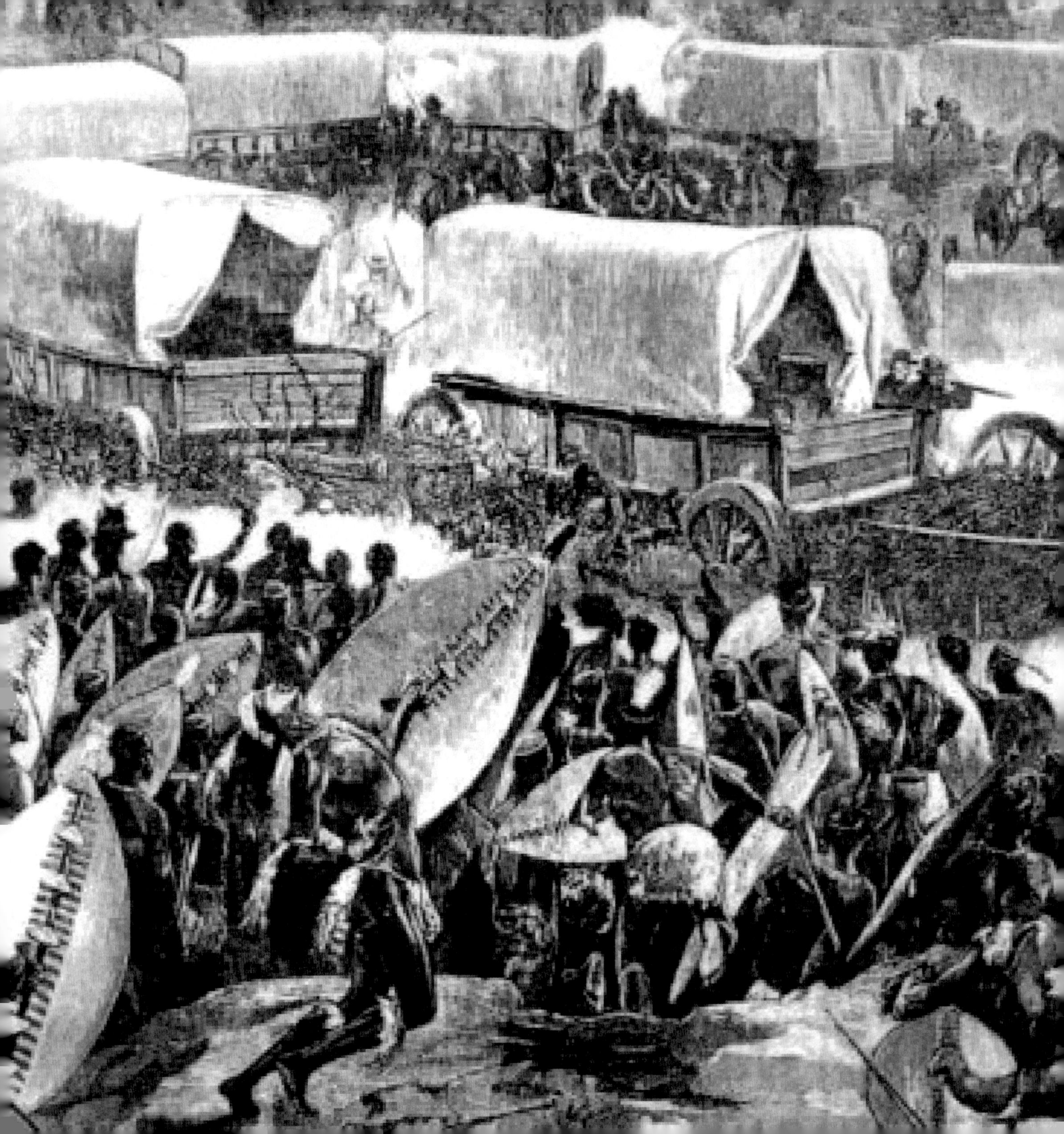

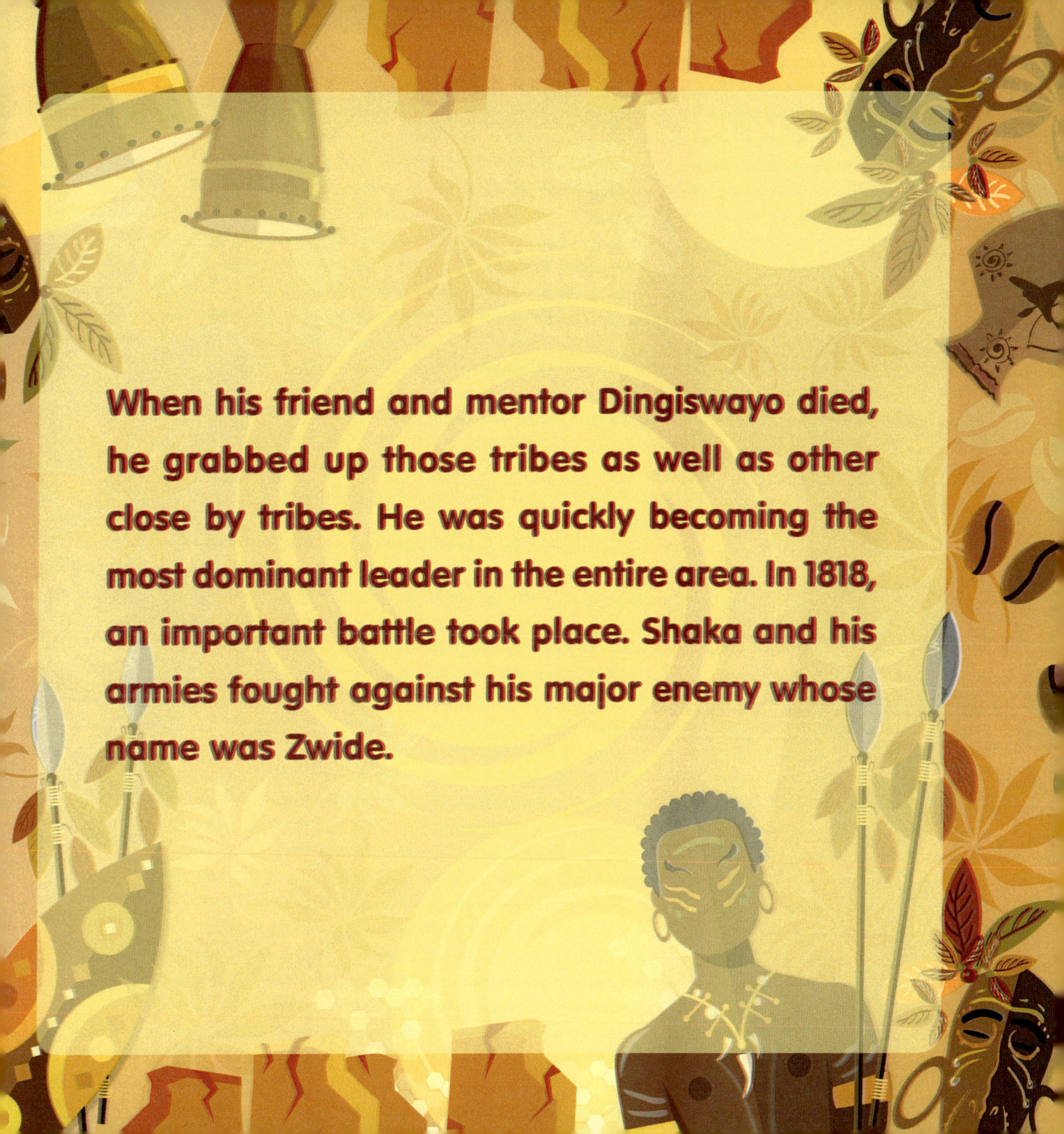

When his friend and mentor Dingiswayo died, he grabbed up those tribes as well as other close by tribes. He was quickly becoming the most dominant leader in the entire area. In 1818, an important battle took place. Shaka and his armies fought against his major enemy whose name was Zwide.

The location of the battle was a place called Gqokli Hill. Although Zwide's army had many more soldiers, Shaka had trained his men well. Their hand-to-hand tactics, weapons, and strategies enabled them to win the battle against their rivals. Now the Zulus were the most important and powerful tribe in all of that region.

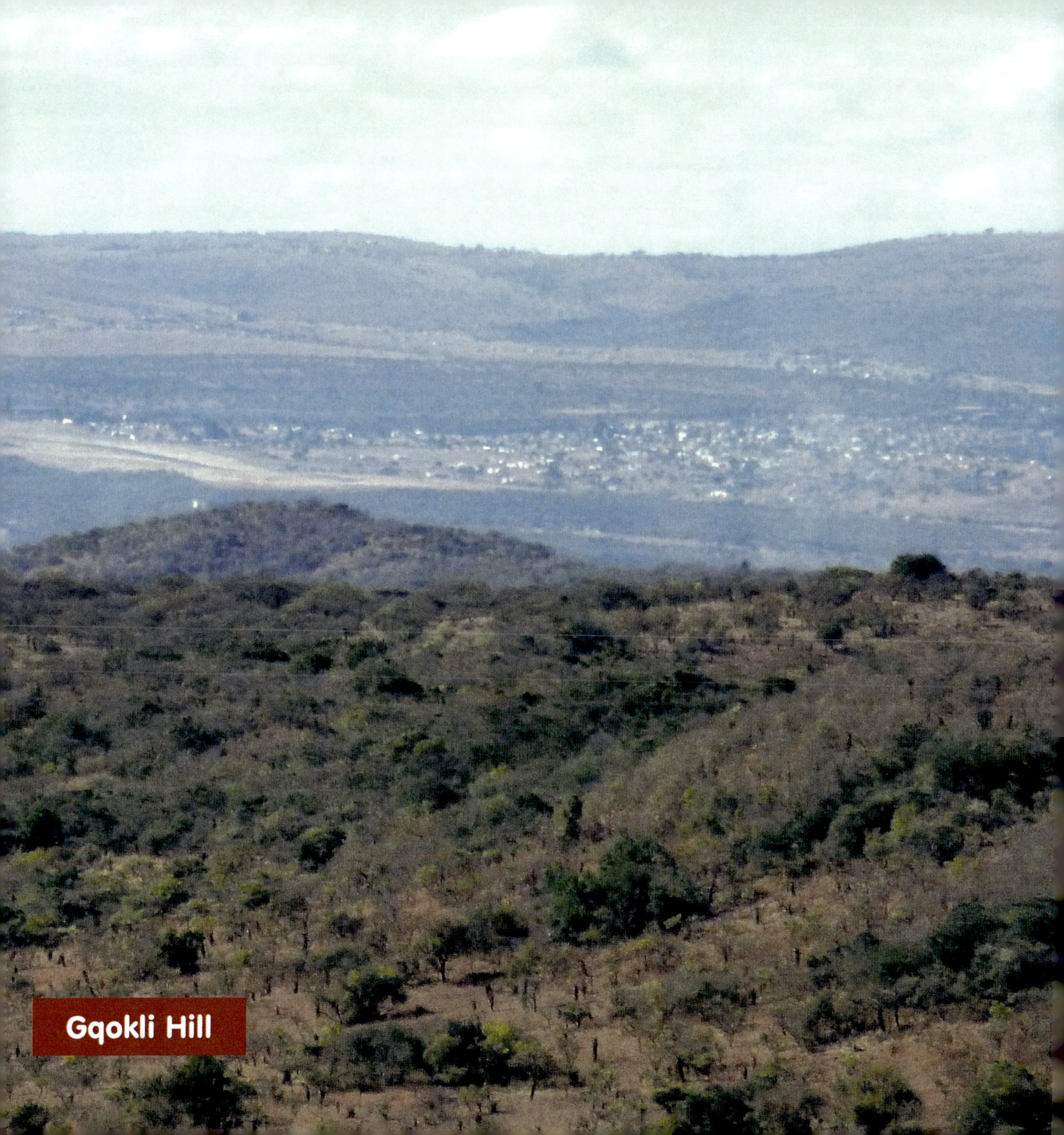
Gqokli Hill

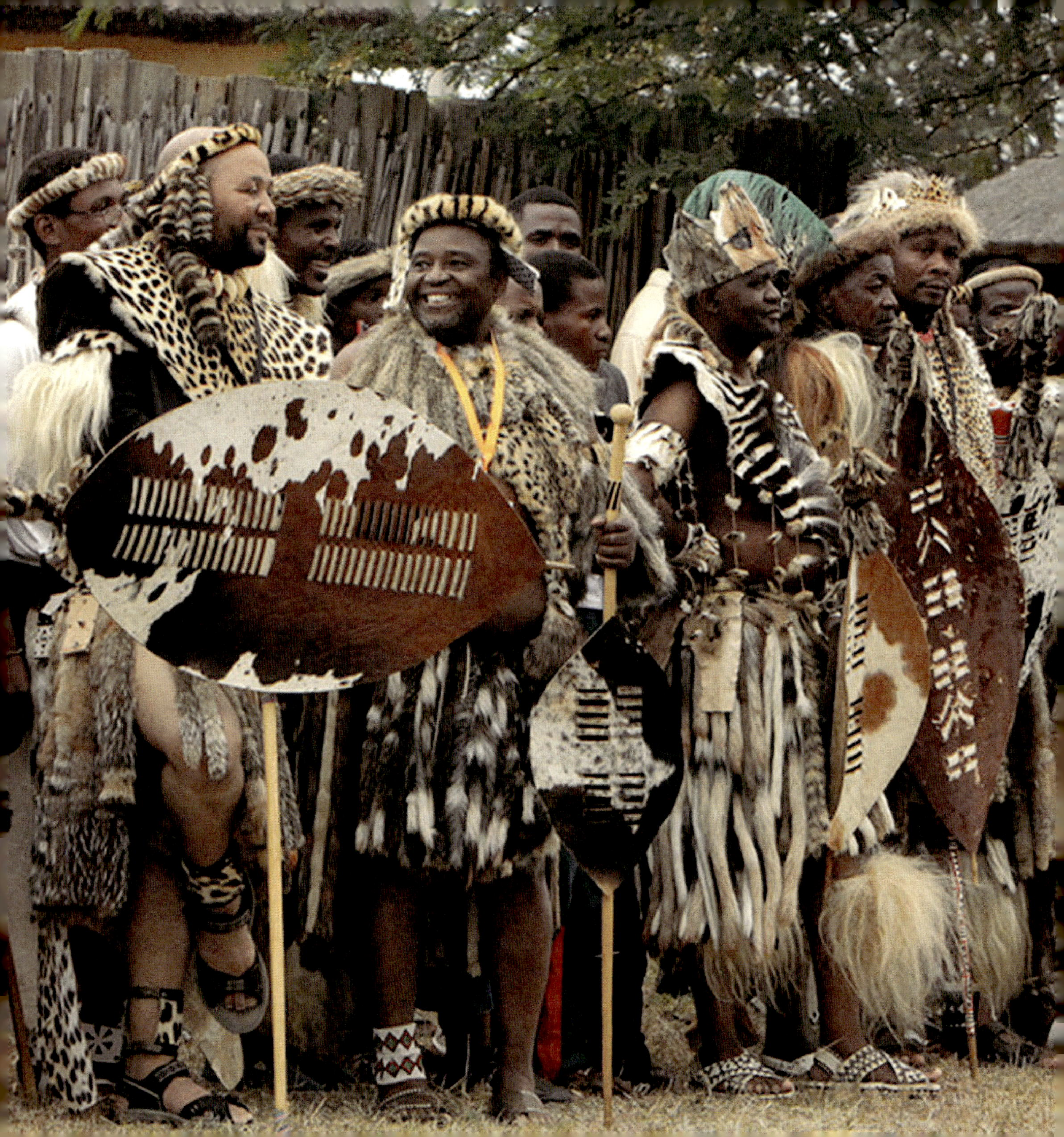

SHAKA'S RISE TO POWER

Shaka had a huge thirst for power. As time went on, he was victorious in battles against other tribal chiefs and won their territories for the Zulus. He continued to build and train his new soldiers to the fighting methods that he had developed. At one time his army consisted of over 40,000 soldiers who had been trained to be fighting machines.

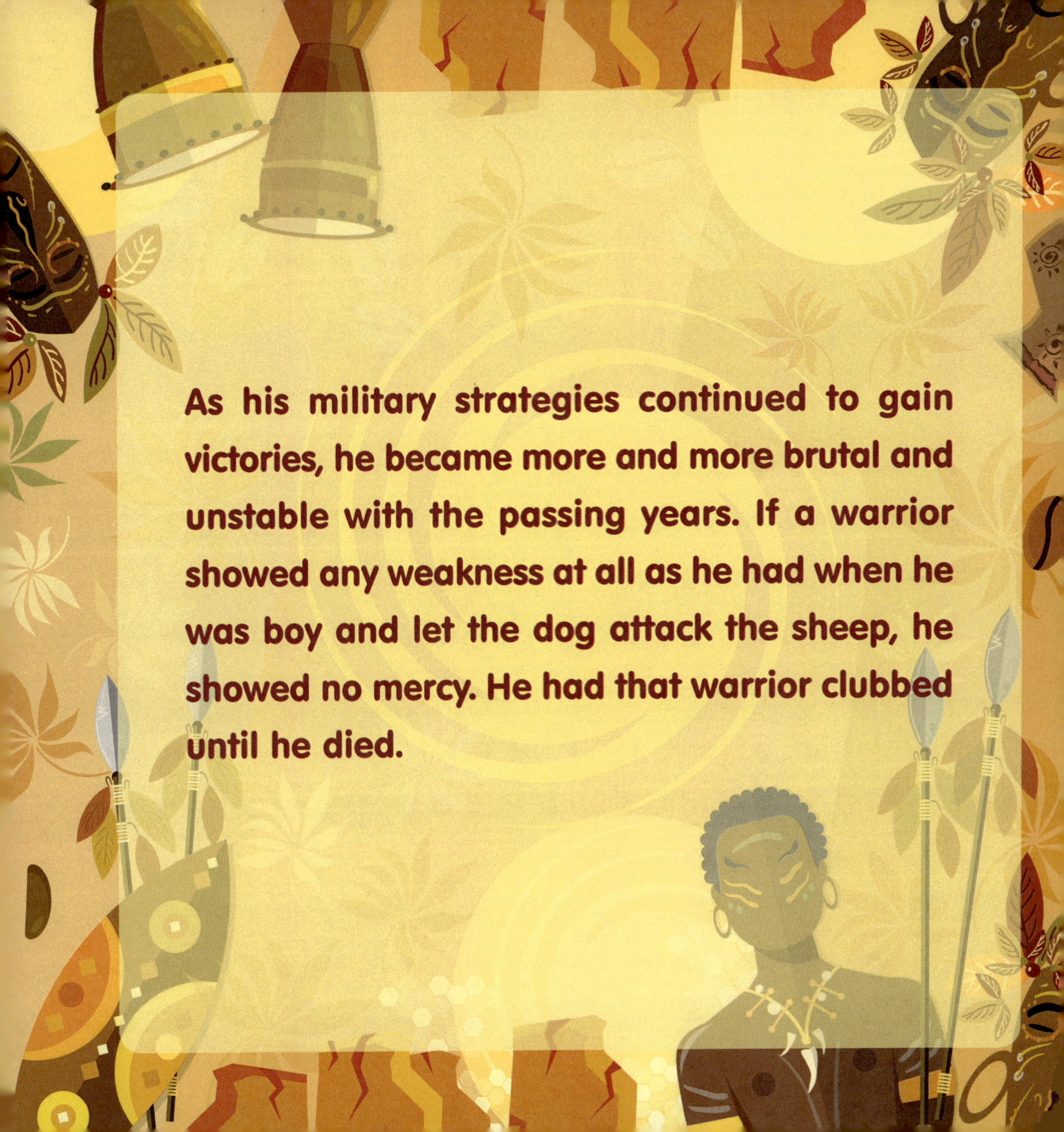

As his military strategies continued to gain victories, he became more and more brutal and unstable with the passing years. If a warrior showed any weakness at all as he had when he was boy and let the dog attack the sheep, he showed no mercy. He had that warrior clubbed until he died.

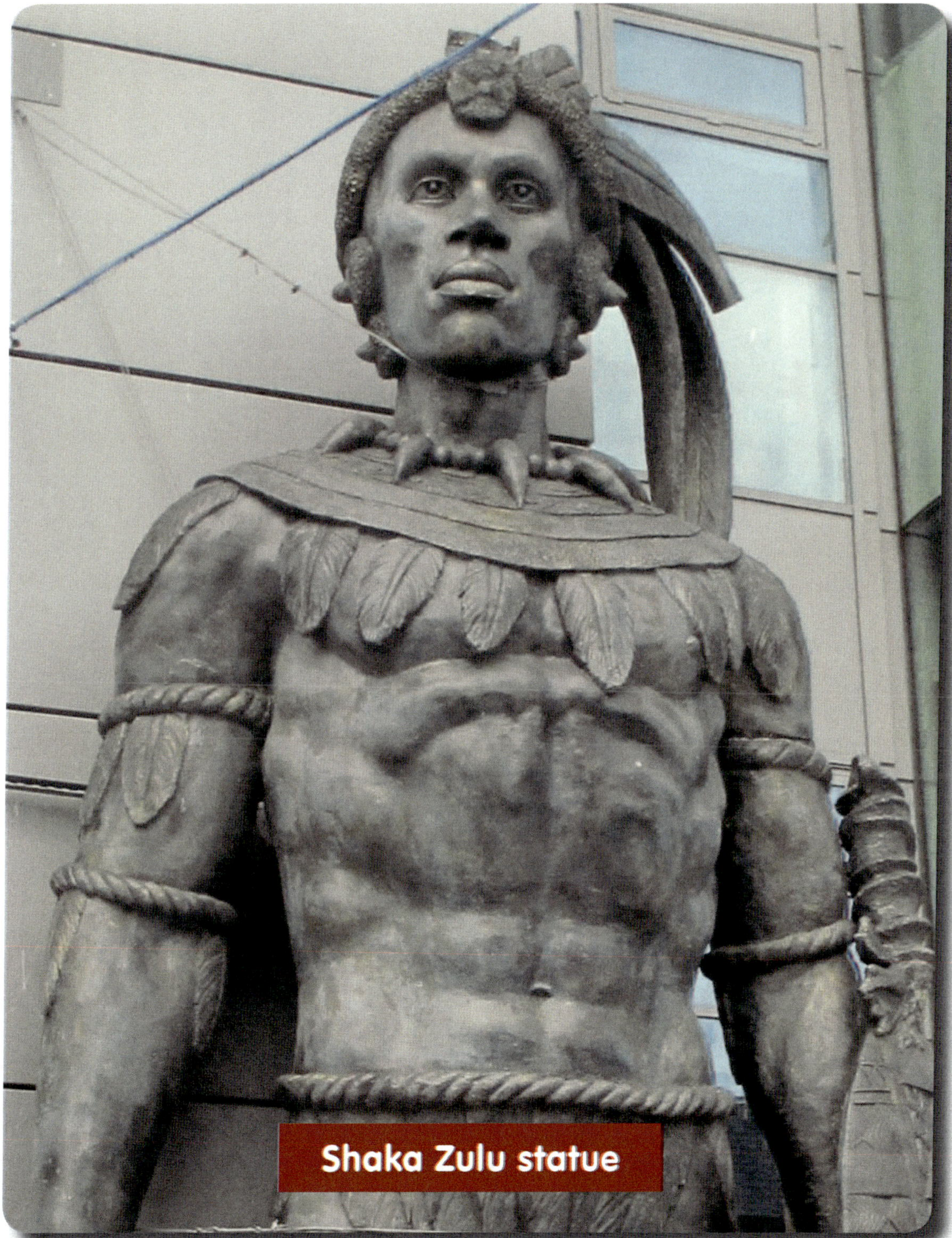

Shaka Zulu statue

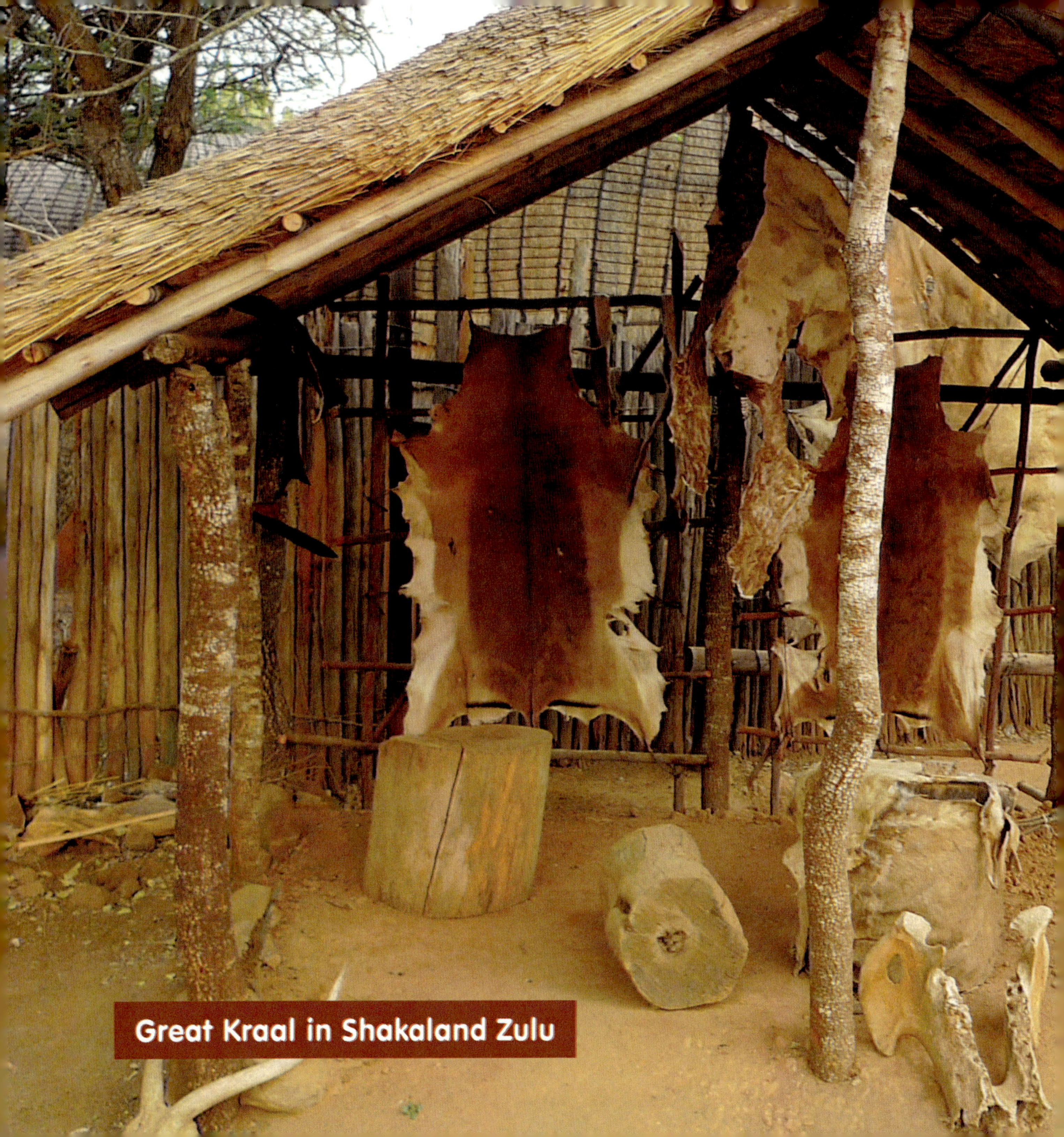

Great Kraal in Shakaland Zulu

Now that his kingdom was so large, he had immense power and he used it in many cases for revenge. He sought out those who had treated him and his mother with disrespect or insults in the past. He then made sure they died very violent deaths.

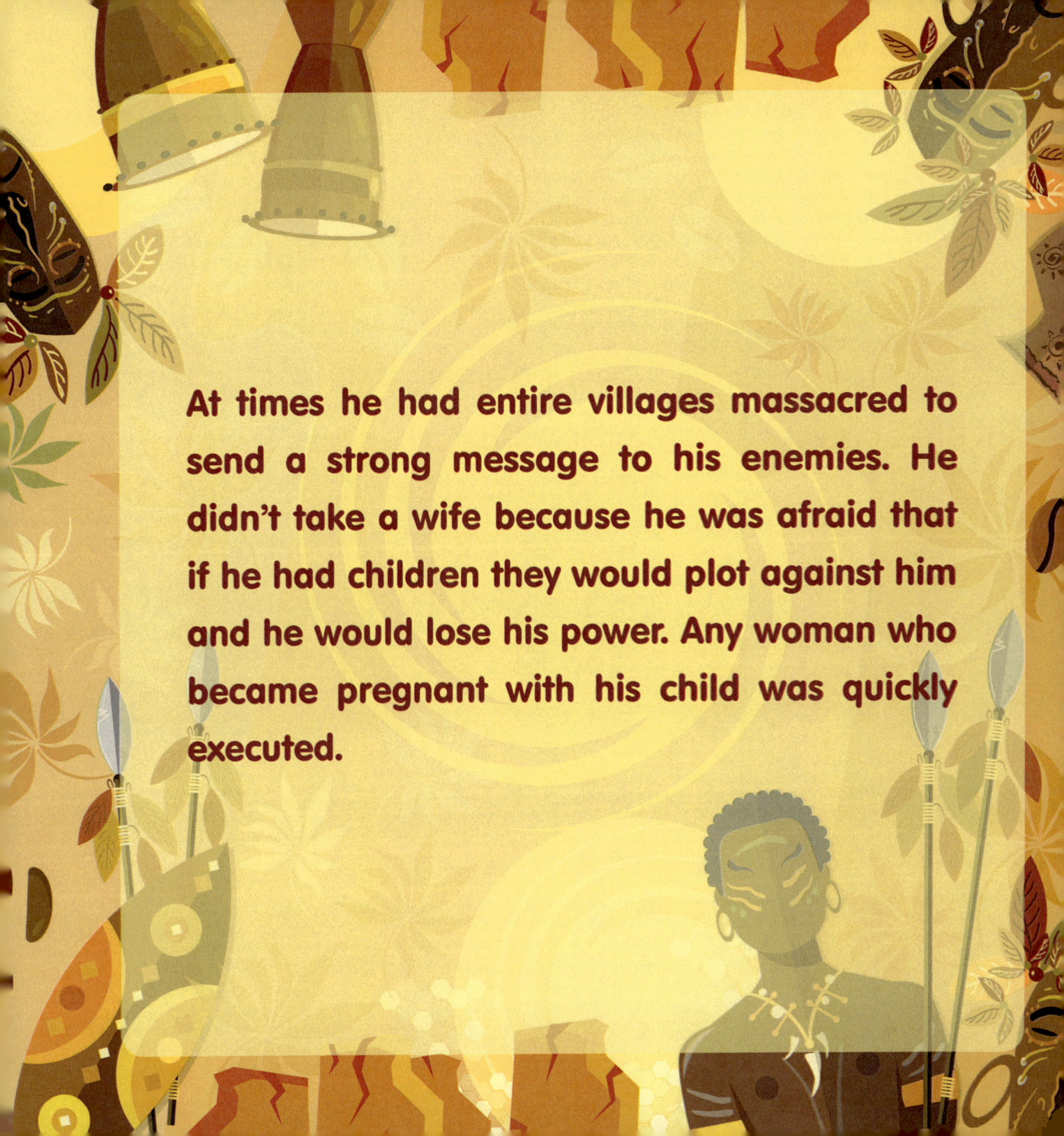

At times he had entire villages massacred to send a strong message to his enemies. He didn't take a wife because he was afraid that if he had children they would plot against him and he would lose his power. Any woman who became pregnant with his child was quickly executed.

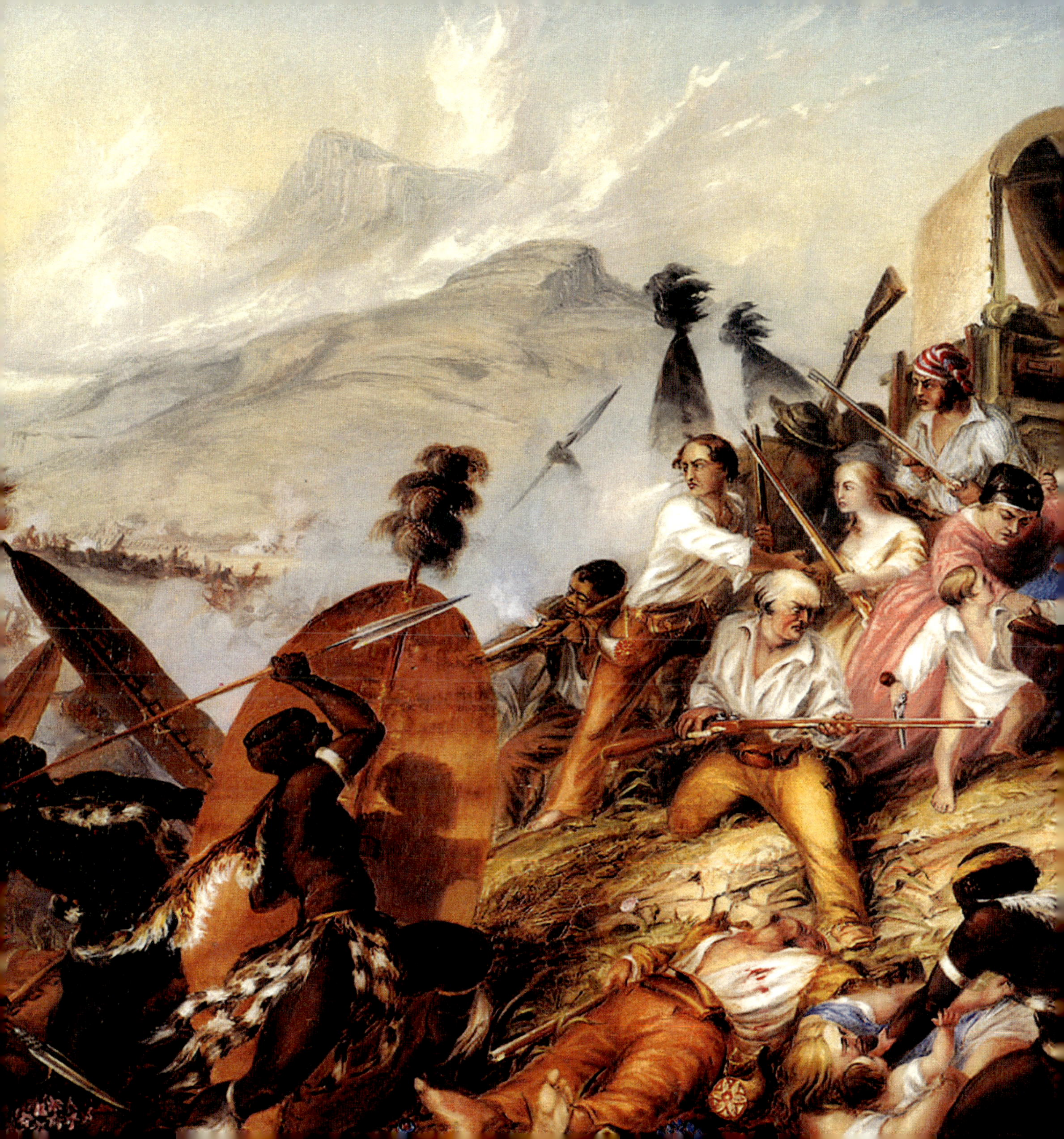

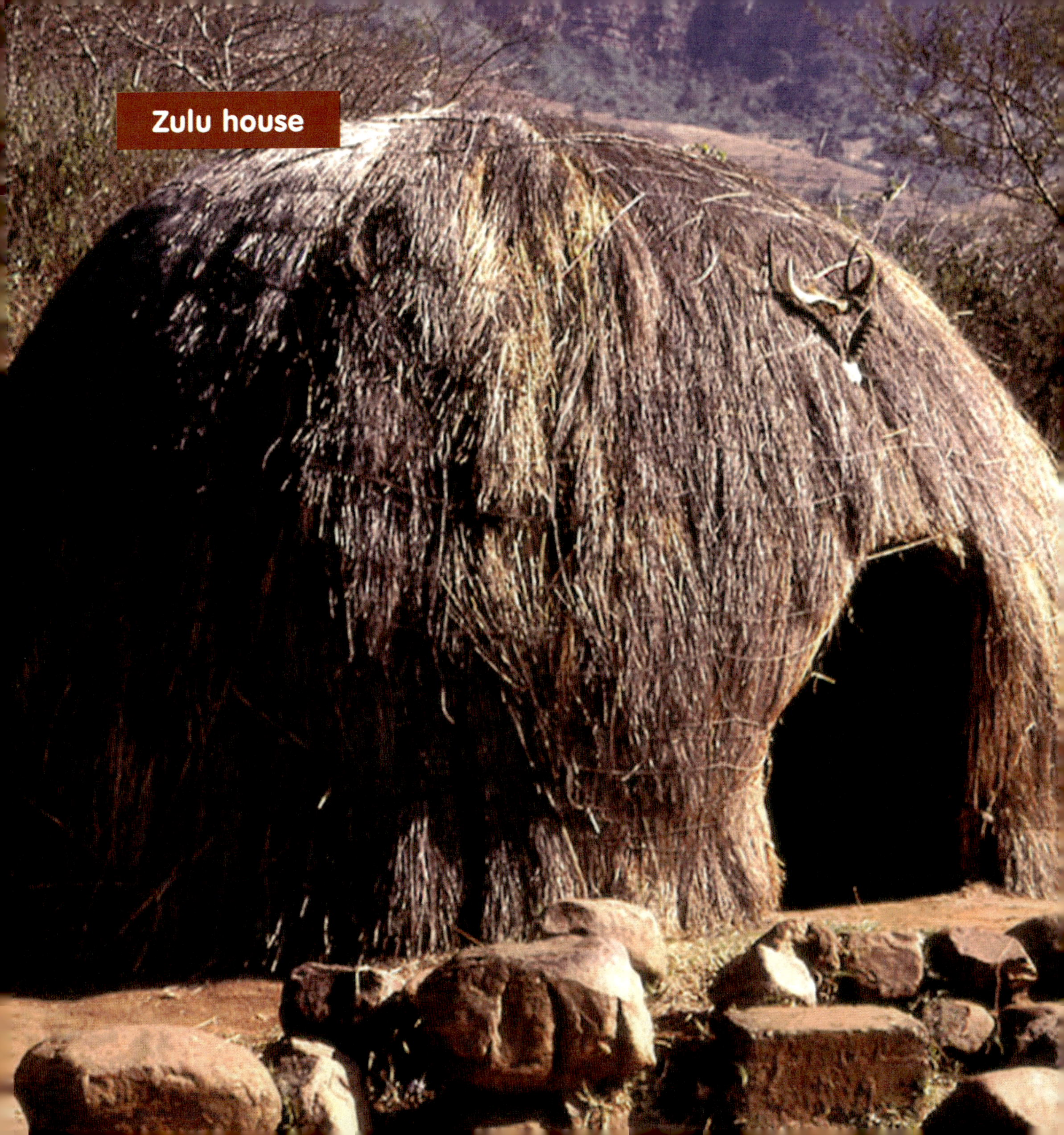
Zulu house

NANDI'S DEATH

As brutal as he was, Shaka loved and was attached to his mother Nandi. When his mother passed away, he felt that the citizens of the kingdom were not mourning as profoundly as they should have. To ensure that they felt his pain, he had many of their family members killed so that they would mourn at the same time he was grieving.

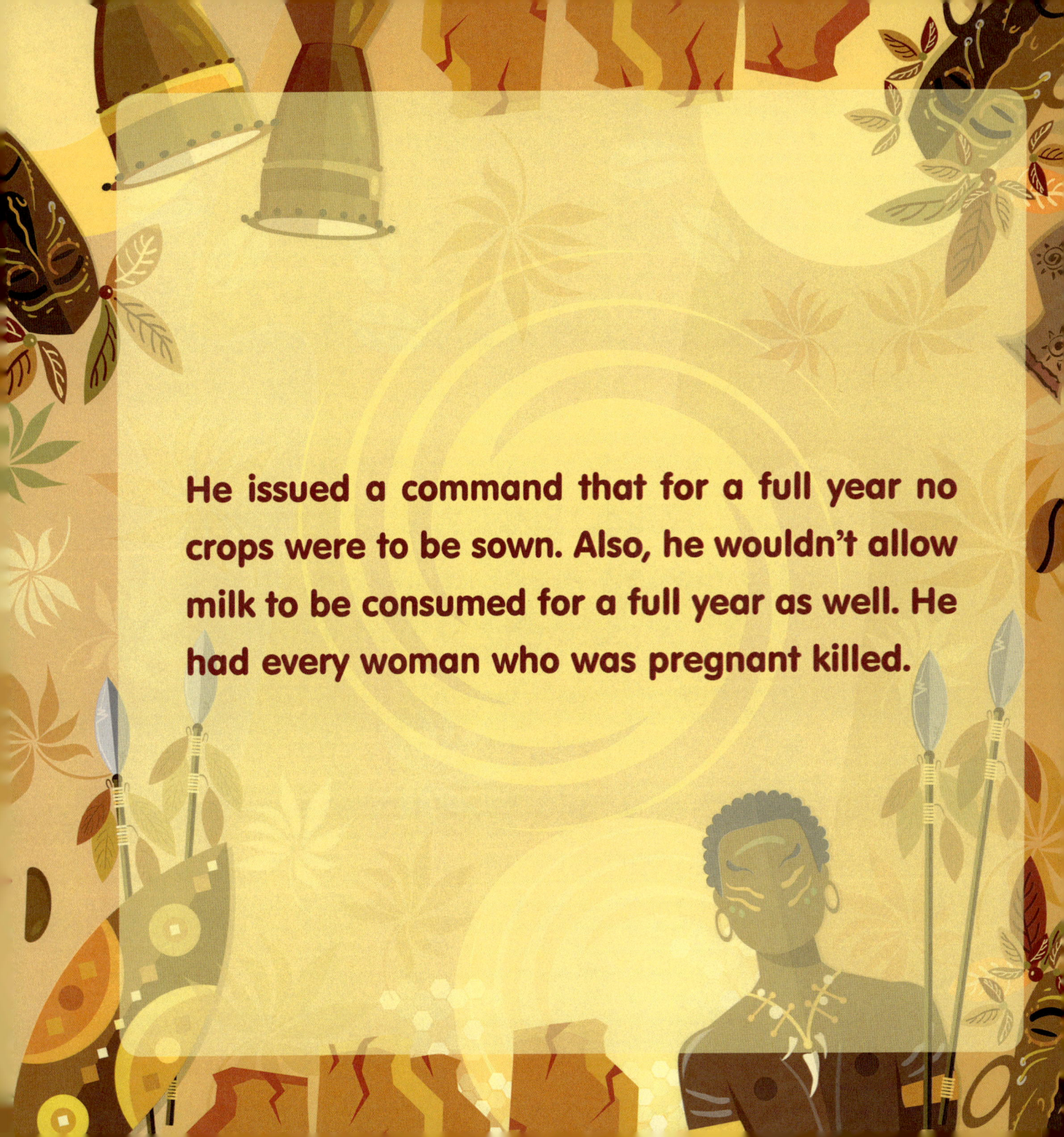

He issued a command that for a full year no crops were to be sown. Also, he wouldn't allow milk to be consumed for a full year as well. He had every woman who was pregnant killed.

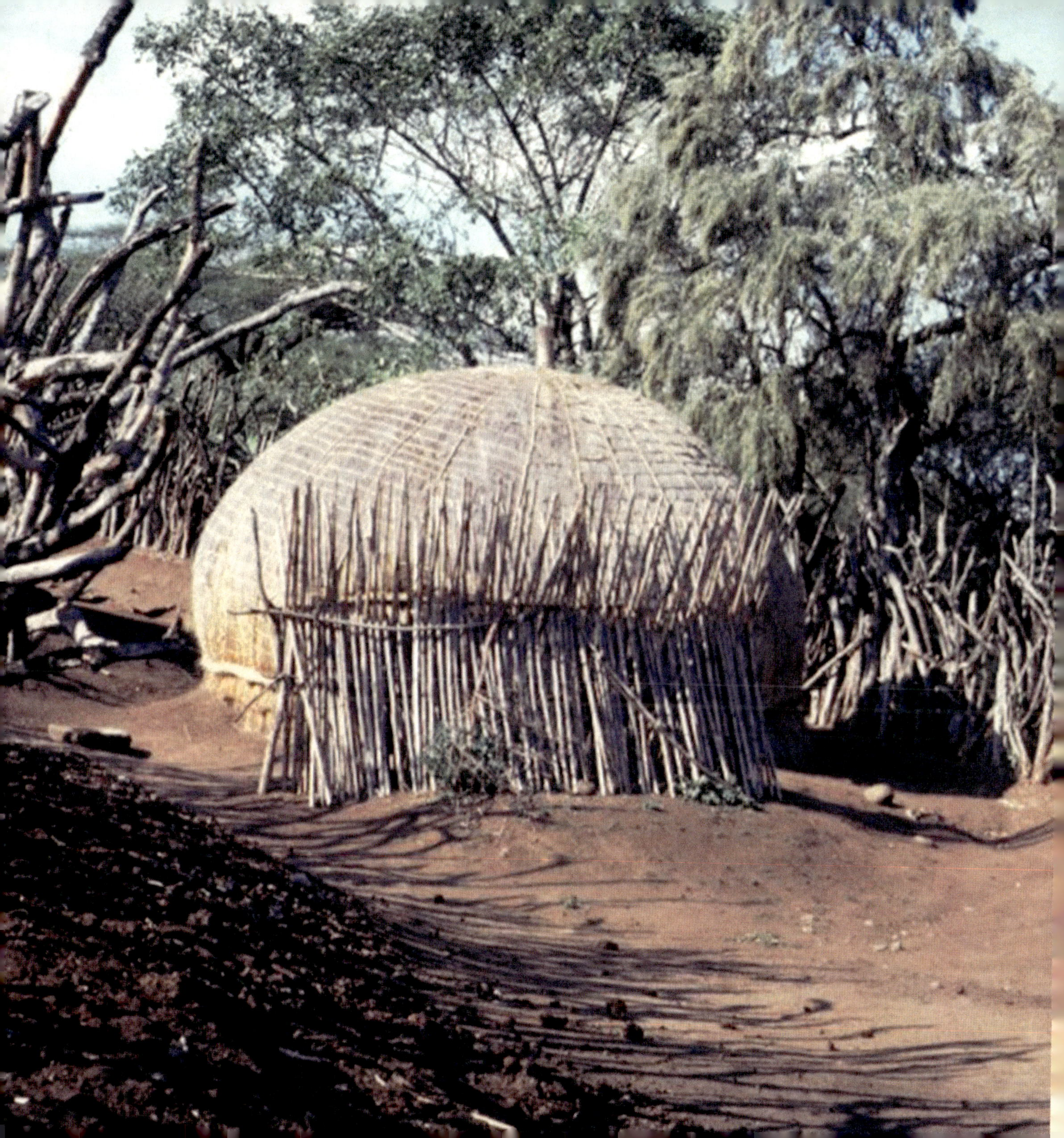

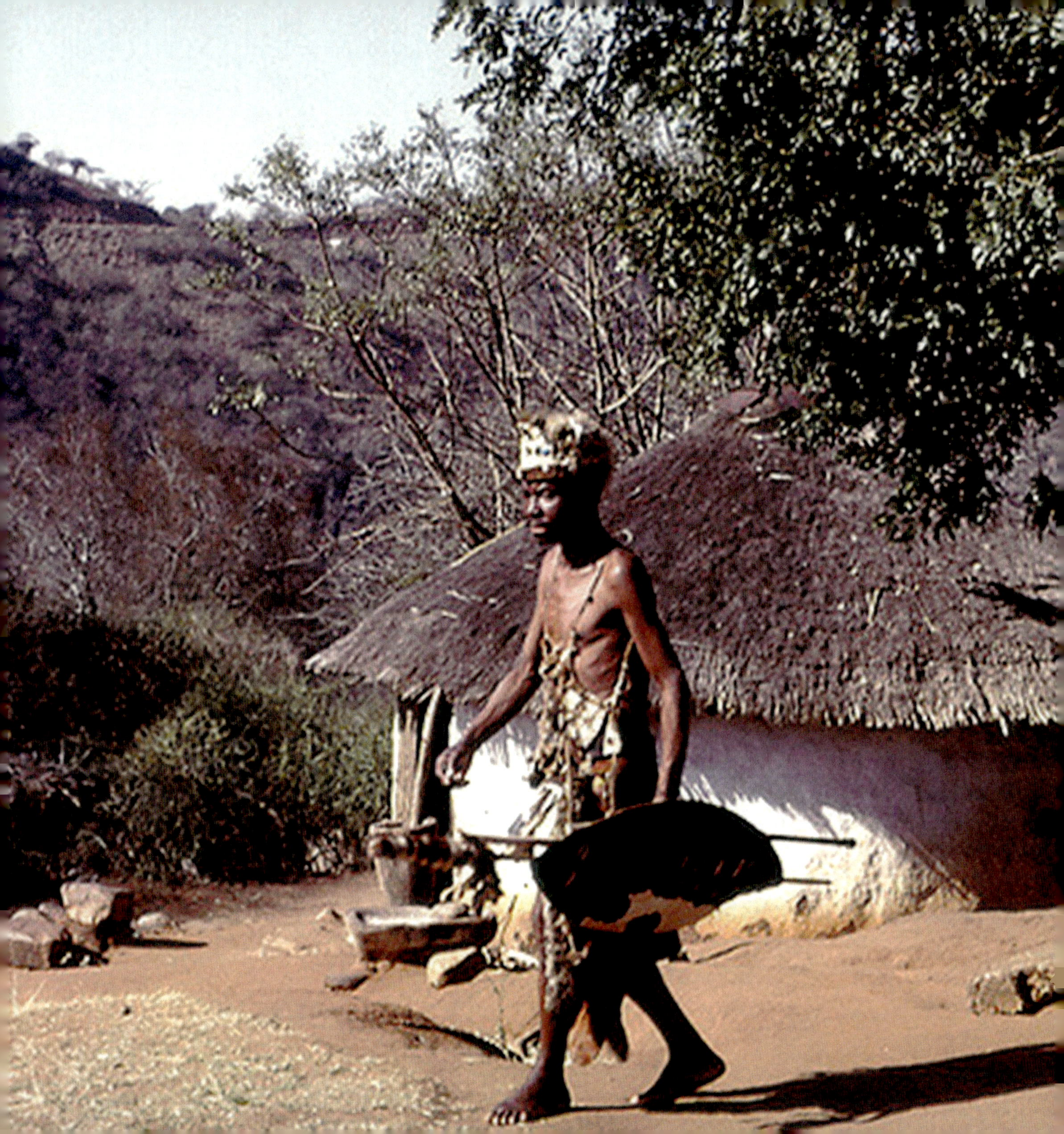

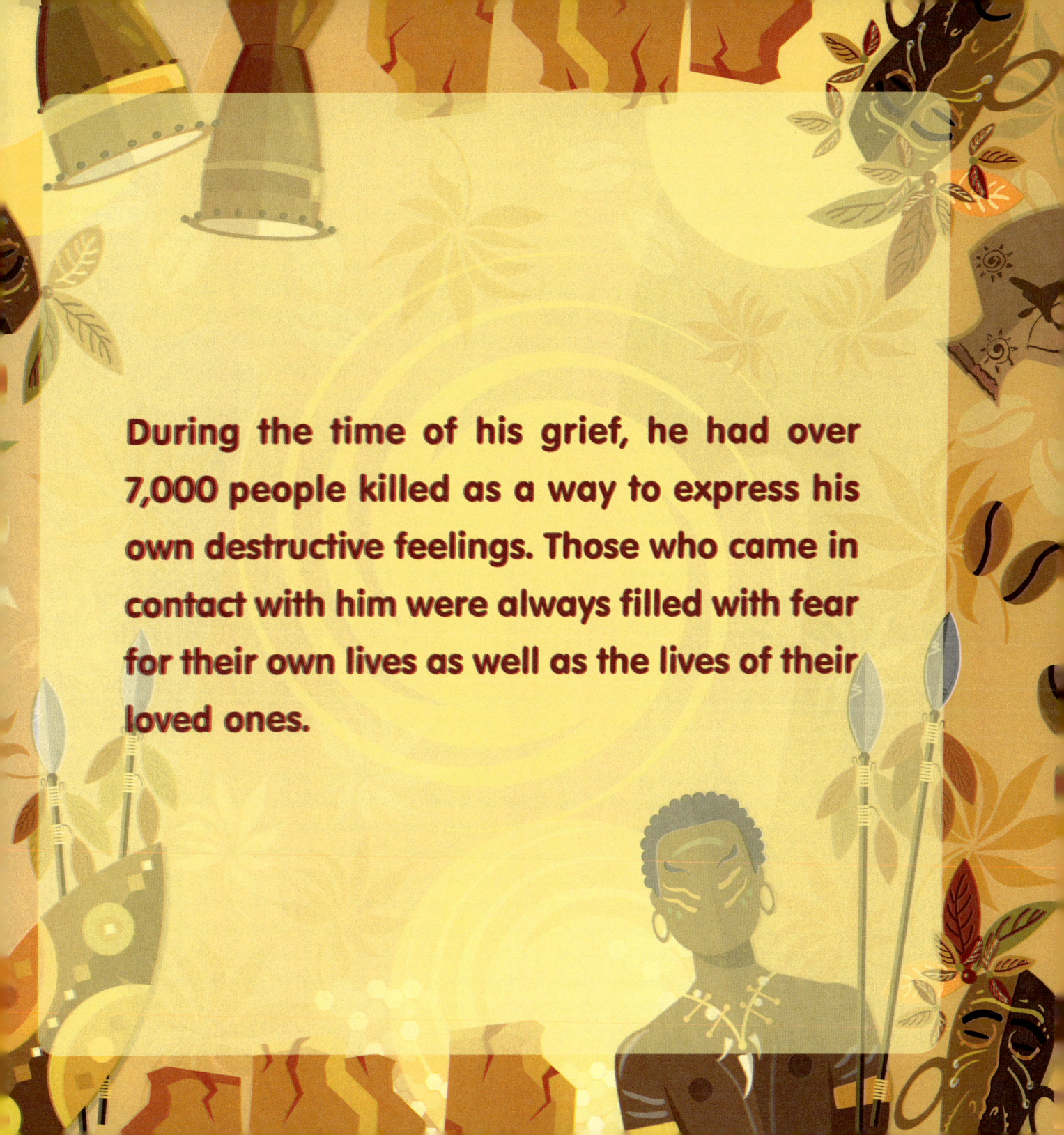

During the time of his grief, he had over 7,000 people killed as a way to express his own destructive feelings. Those who came in contact with him were always filled with fear for their own lives as well as the lives of their loved ones.

SHAKA'S DEATH

Shaka's fears came true when his half-brother by the name of Dingawe killed him and threw his body into an unmarked pit. Dingawe took the throne.

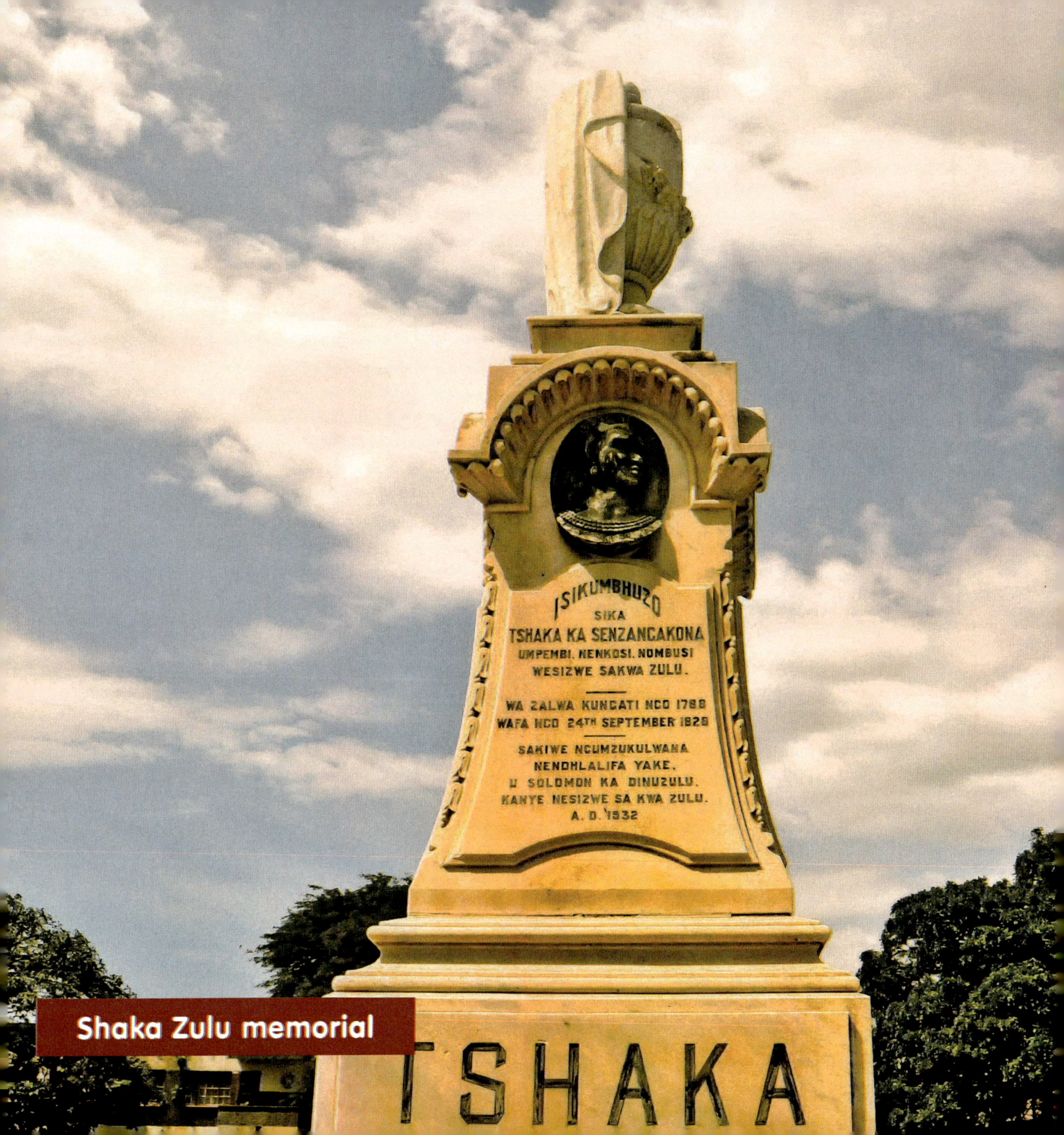
ISIKUMBHUZO
SIKA
TSHAKA KA SENZANGAKONA
UMPEMBI, NENKOSI, NOMBUSI
WESIZWE SAKWA ZULU.
WA ZALWA KUNGATI NGO 1788
WAFA NGO 24TH SEPTEMBER 1828
SAKIWE NGUMZUKULWANA
NENDHLALIFA YAKE.
U SOLOMON KA DINUZULU.
KANYE NESIZWE SA KWA ZULU.
A. D. 1932
TSHAKA
Shaka Zulu memorial

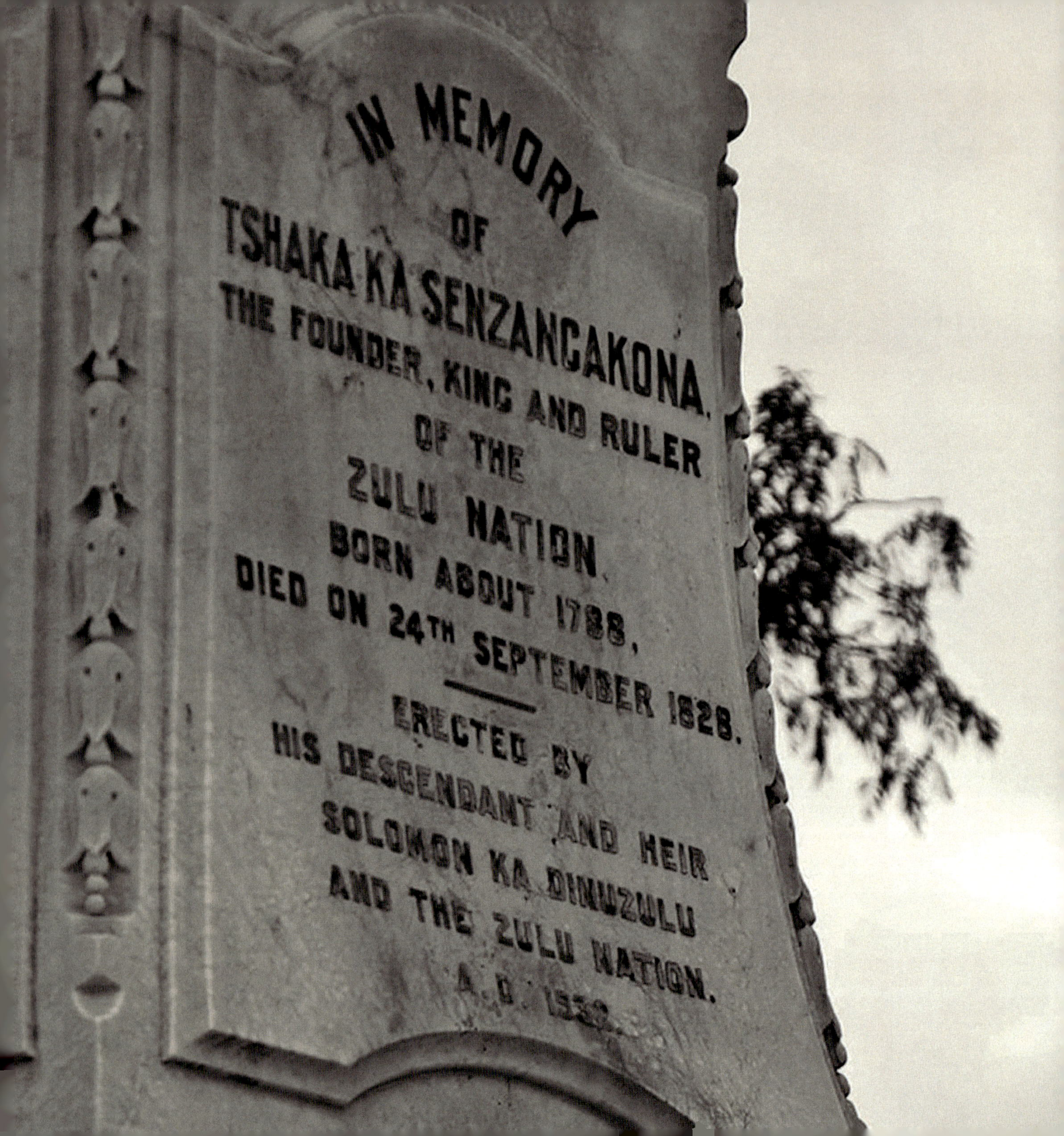
IN MEMORY
OF
TSHAKA KA SENZANGAKONA.
THE FOUNDER, KING AND RULER
OF THE
ZULU NATION.
BORN ABOUT 1788.
DIED ON 24TH SEPTEMBER 1828.
ERECTED BY
HIS DESCENDANT AND HEIR
SOLOMON KA DINUZULU
AND THE ZULU NATION.
A.D.

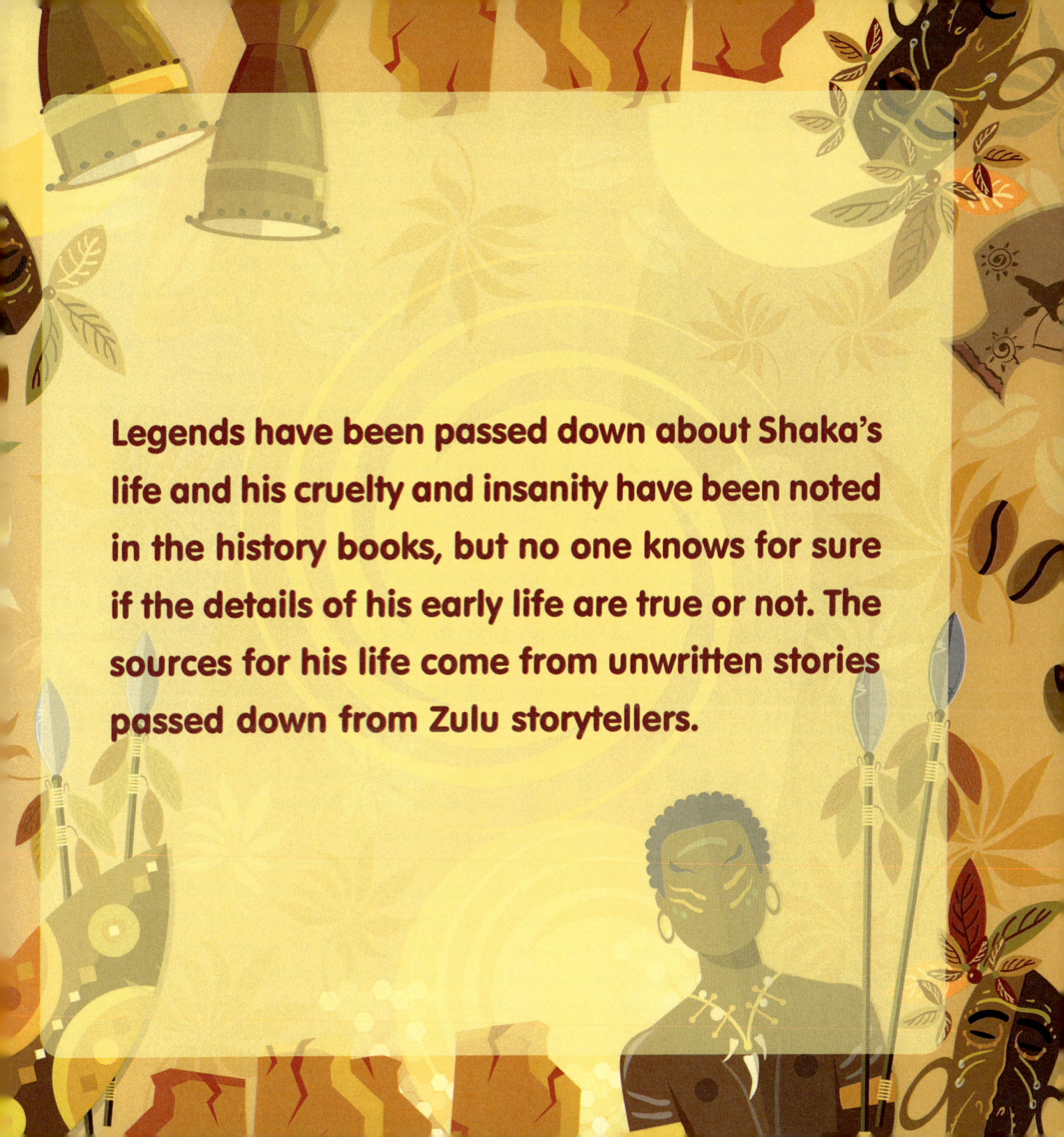

Legends have been passed down about Shaka's life and his cruelty and insanity have been noted in the history books, but no one knows for sure if the details of his early life are true or not. The sources for his life come from unwritten stories passed down from Zulu storytellers.

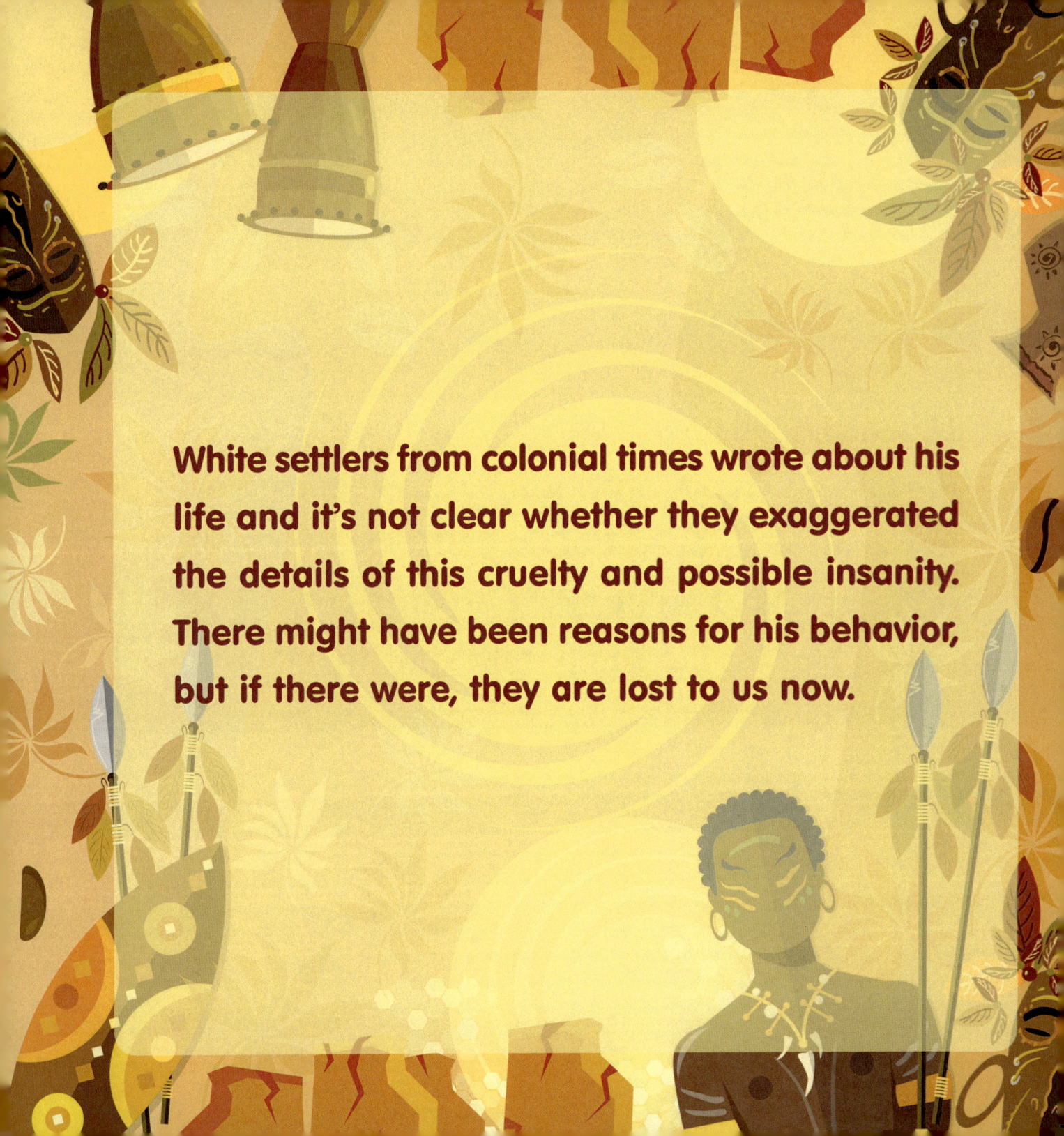

White settlers from colonial times wrote about his life and it's not clear whether they exaggerated the details of this cruelty and possible insanity. There might have been reasons for his behavior, but if there were, they are lost to us now.

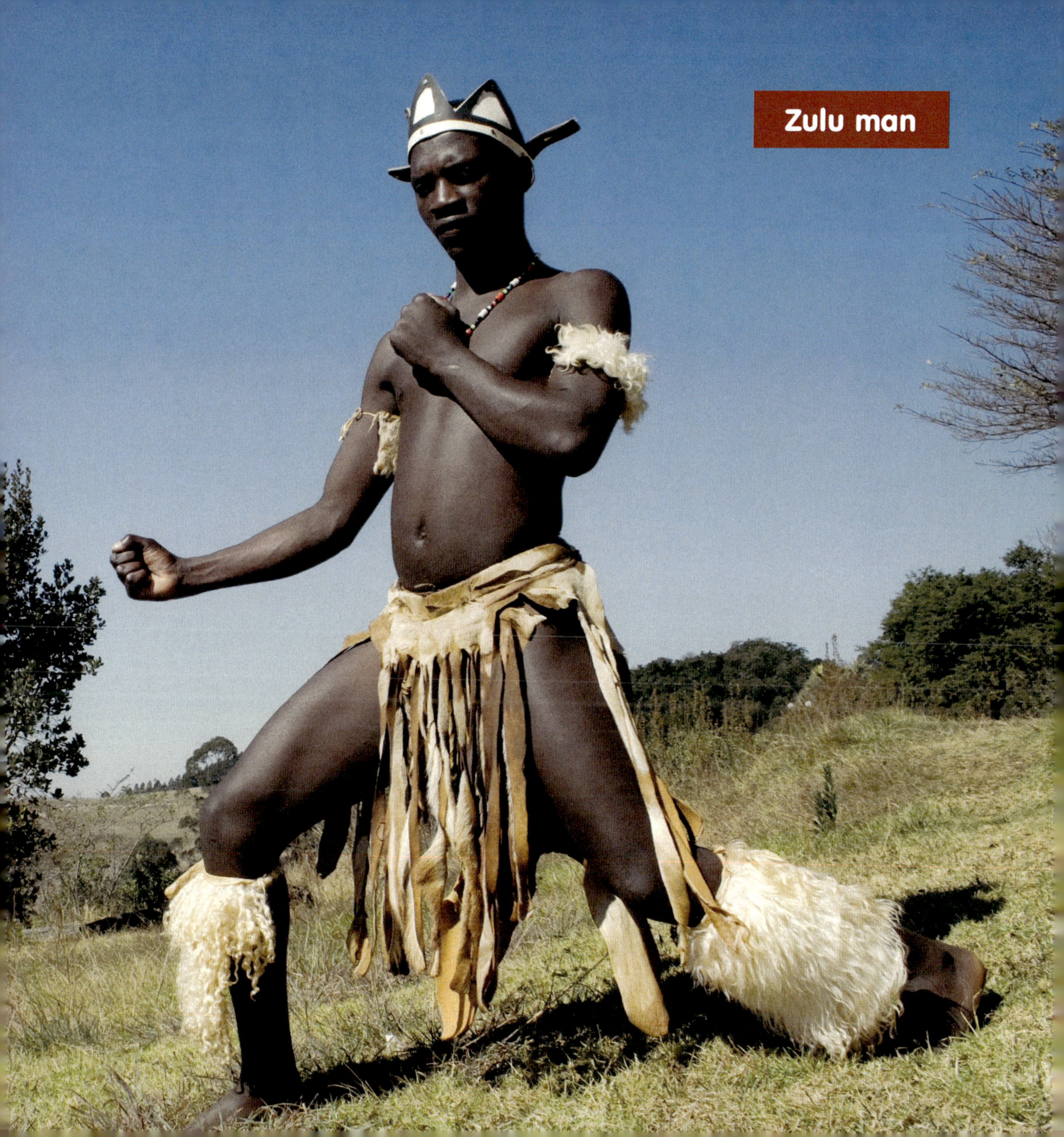
Zulu man

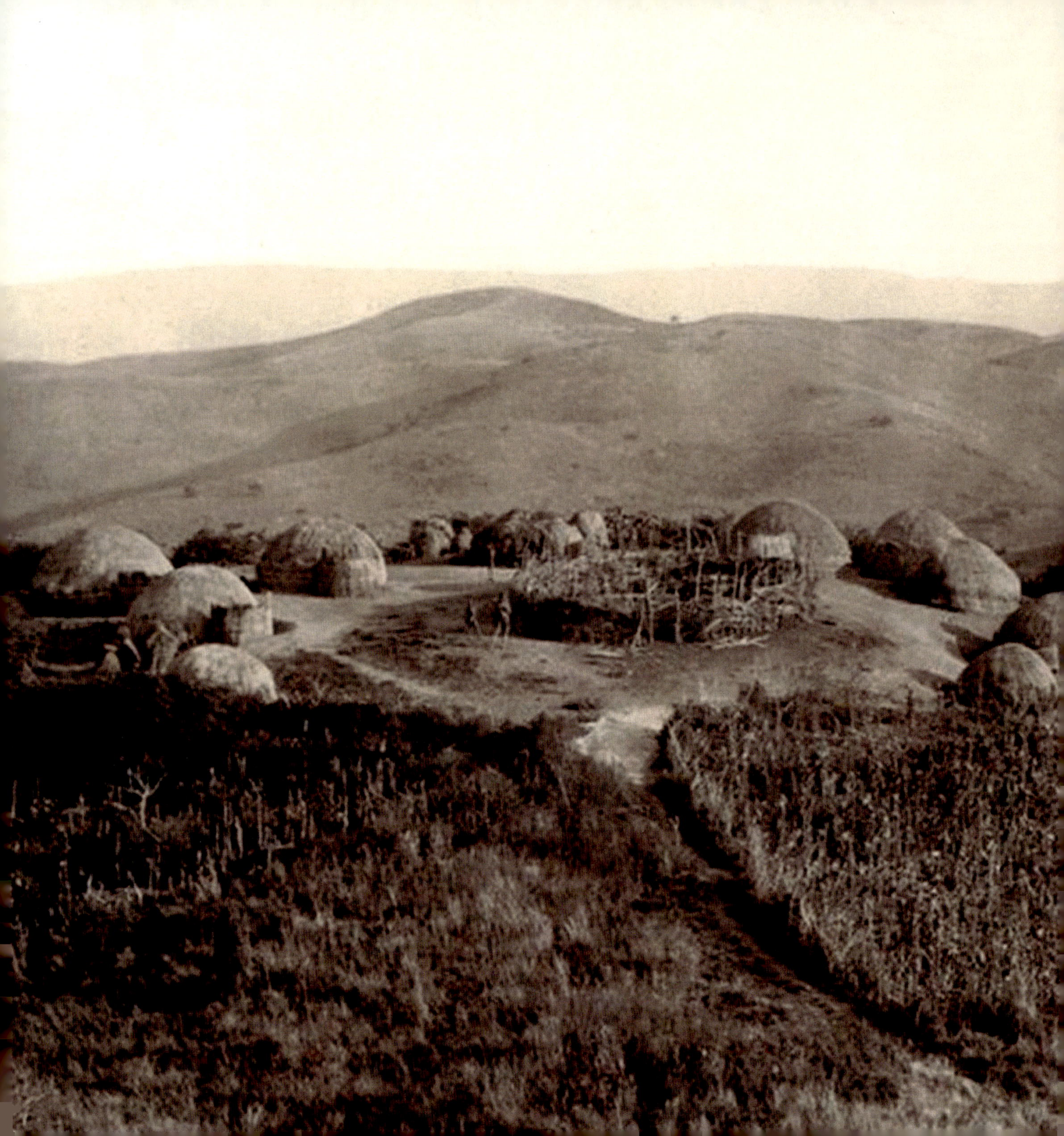

FASCINATING FACTS ABOUT SHAKA ZULU

- In order to free up his soldiers to focus only on fighting, he hired young boys to carry the needed military supplies.
- He forced his soldiers to fight barefoot as he had fought. As a result, none of his soldiers were allowed to wear sandals.
- His soldiers were not given permission to marry until they had been victorious in battle. He wanted them to sacrifice in order to get what they wanted.
- The capital of his kingdom was named Bulawayo, which translates to "the location where the people are massacred."

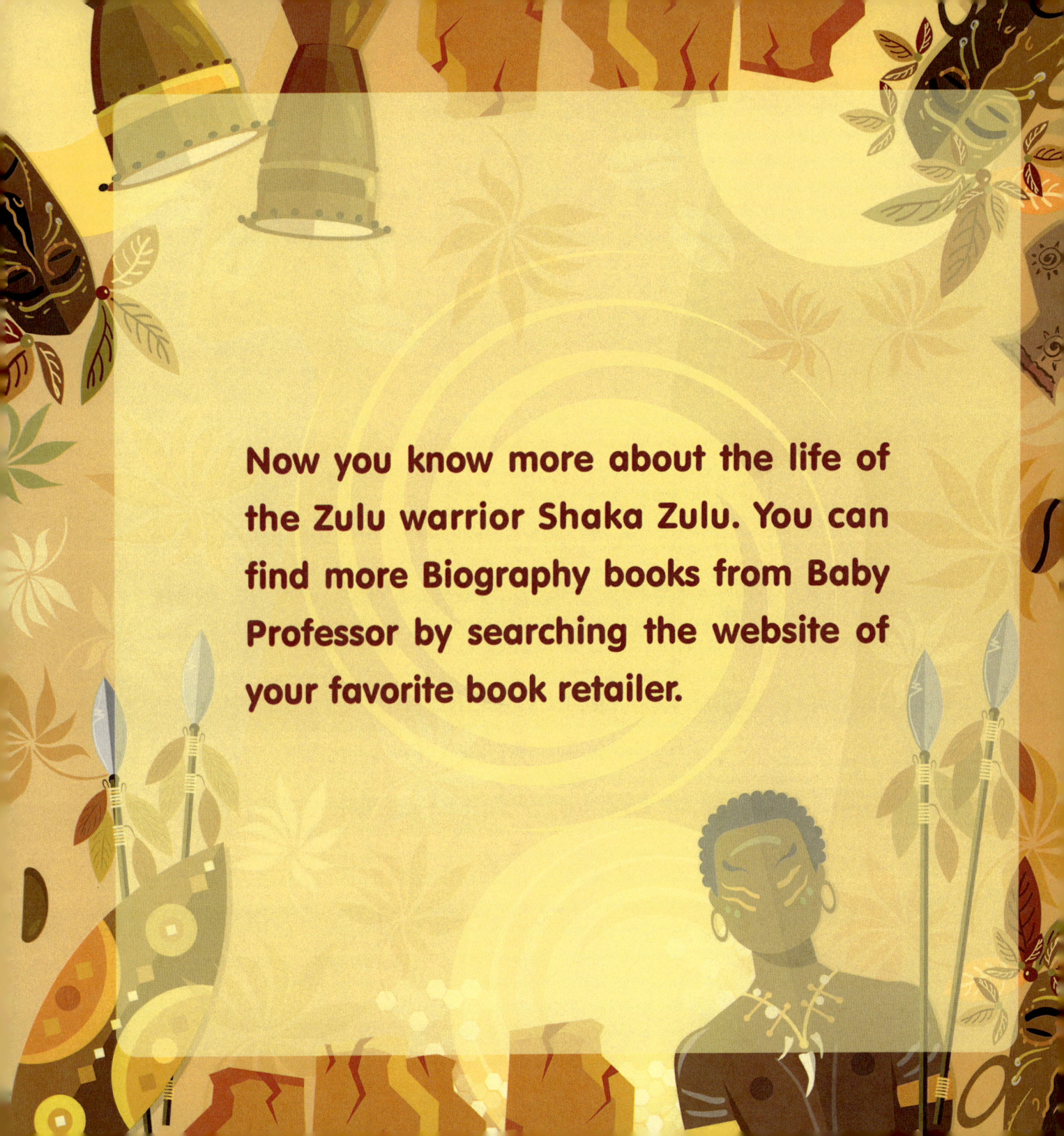

Now you know more about the life of the Zulu warrior Shaka Zulu. You can find more Biography books from Baby Professor by searching the website of your favorite book retailer.

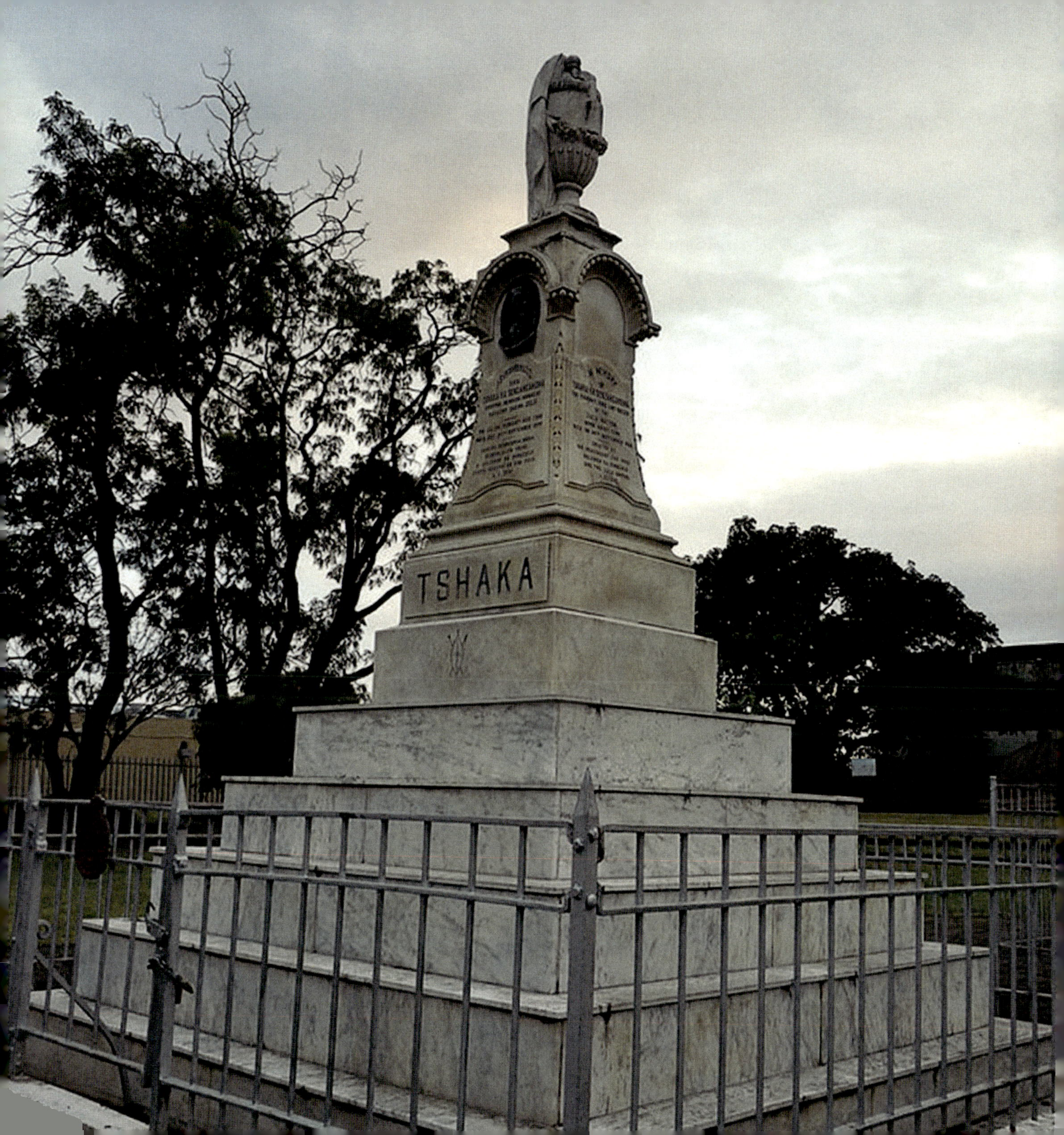
TSHAKA

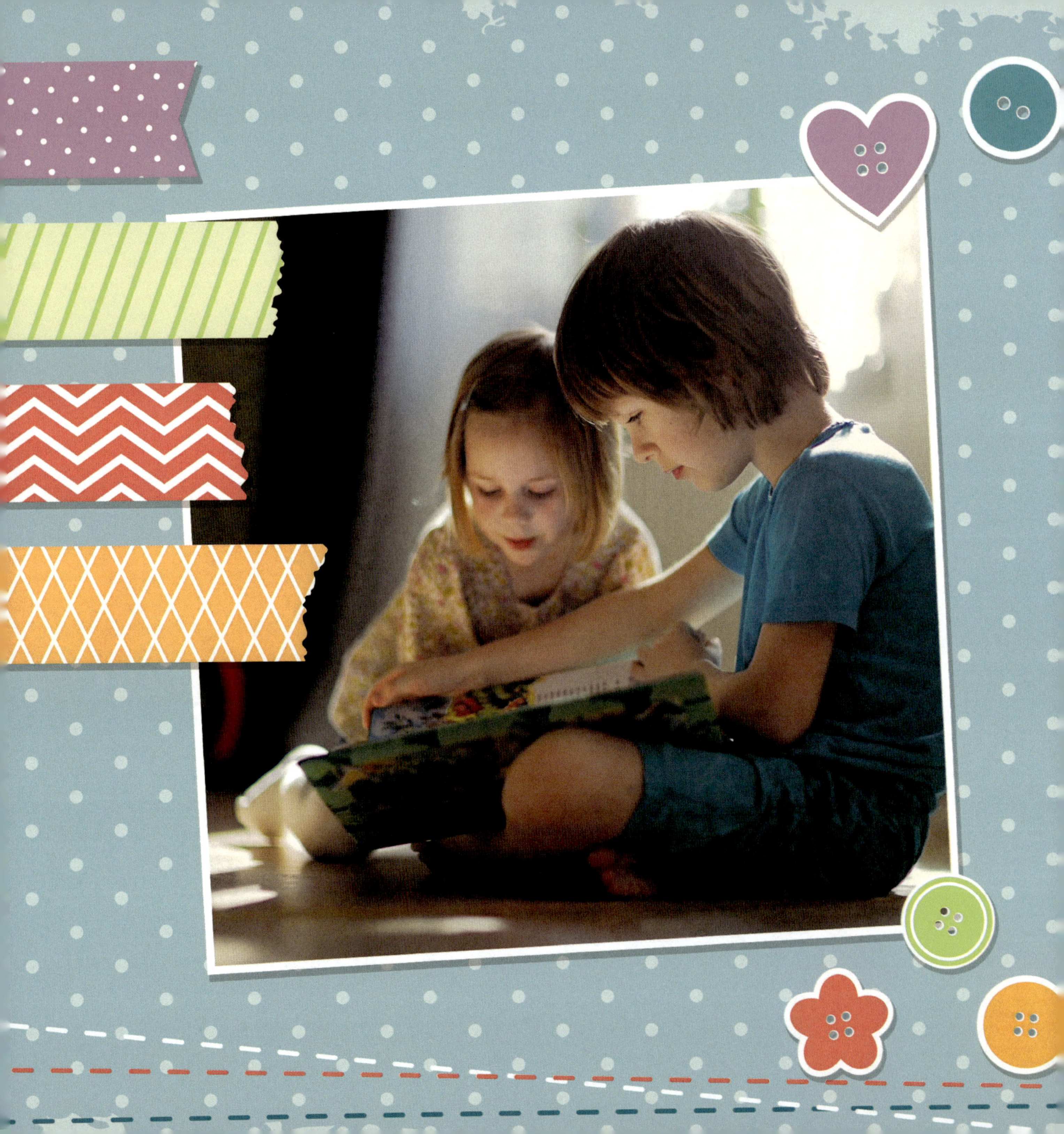

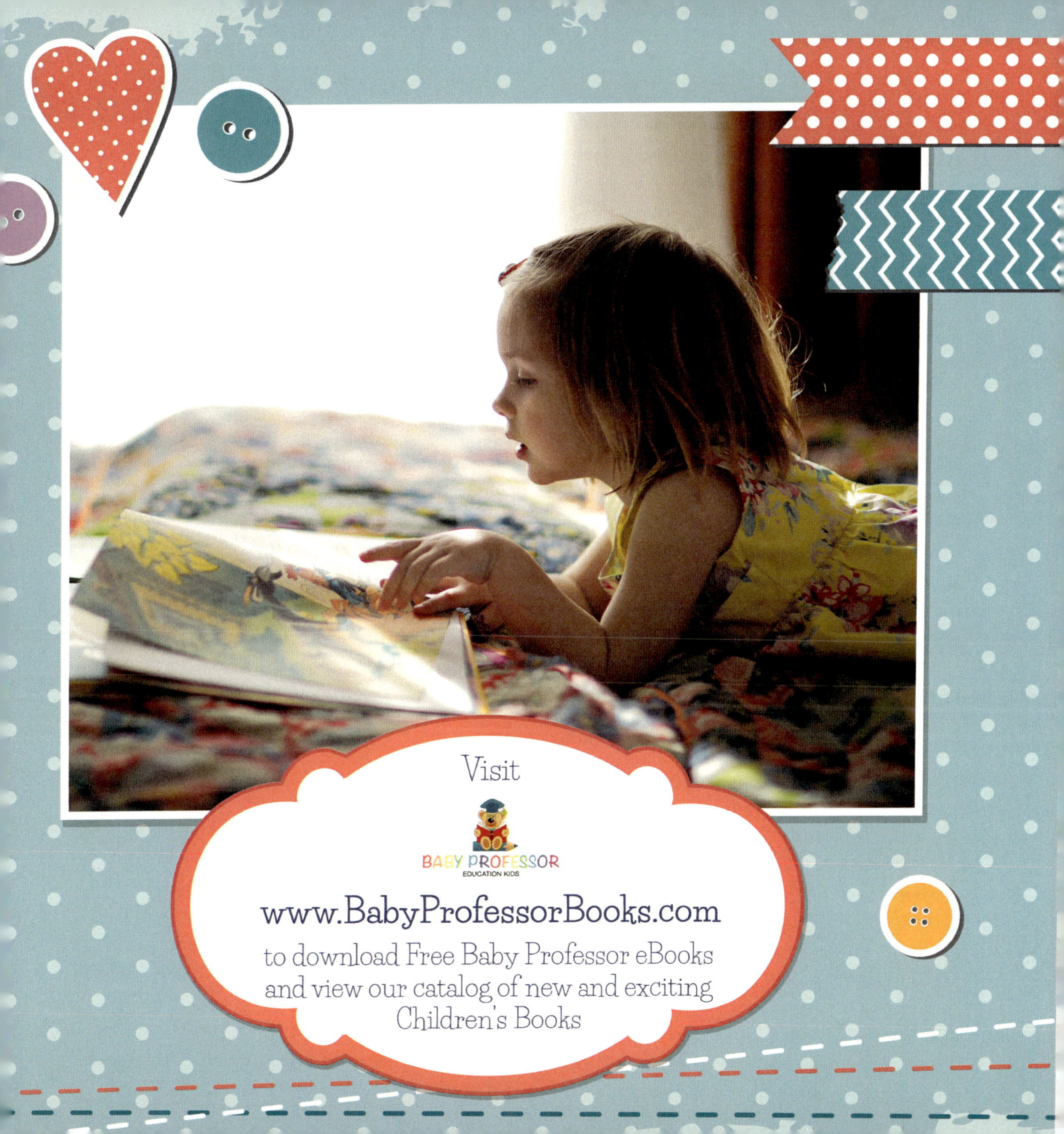

Made in the USA
Las Vegas, NV
27 September 2023

78215204R00040